Data Protection and Privacy Implementation -India Perspective

Prof RK Dubey

Ajay Kumar Verma

Copyright © 2019 Ajay Kumar Verma

All rights reserved.

ISBN: 9781712746356

FOREWORD

Kiran Karnik*

The extraordinary progress in the development – and, even more so, in the deployment – of new information and communication technologies (ICT) has brought about rapid changes in the operations of both business and government. Nowhere is this more visible than in India. In this millennium, and especially over the last decade, a series of policies and new technologies has taken the country to the forefront of those leveraging digital technologies for leap-frogging into a new world. With 1.2 billion mobile devices, and telecom coverage extending to nearly the full population, India has become a 'connected nation'. A digital identity for practically all Indians, through Aadhar, bank accounts with a linkage to Aadhar and to mobile phone numbers, digital money transfer via phone apps: all this, and more, has transformed life for all – most visibly for the hundreds of millions of disadvantaged Indians. Direct bank transfer (DBT) of money into individual bank accounts for subsidies, pensions, scholarships, loans, etc. has greatly reduced leakages and corruption. Withdrawal of money from one's account can now be done through a local functionary (the 'bank correspondent') – no need of going to a bank, or even an ATM; similarly, money transfer to other accounts can be done without visiting a bank, over a phone through UPI.

Along with this, other transactions such as e-commerce, food delivery and taxi hire services, are done digitally at all stages: from order to payment. Meanwhile, a host of new apps have been launched, even as many existing ones have vastly expanded their reach. Most of these – such as WhatsApp, Facebook or Tiktok – are free, but require one to register and, as part of that, provide some data.

This rapid digitalisation of a large economy and the resulting transactions – registering, buying, selling, down-loading, and paying – generate massive amounts of data. This includes a great deal of an individual's personal and sensitive data (e.g., credit card and bank account numbers, Aadhar, address, health data, etc.).

A popular refrain is 'data is the new oil'. This is not quite so, for - unlike oil - data is non-depleting, shareable, not geographically rooted, and often loses value with time. Also, unlike oil, multiple people/entities can draw benefits from the same data, and so sharing is not a zero-sum game. Yet, the phrase is apt to the extent it indicates value. Data is, indeed, the raw material which, when mined and analysed, can provide deep insights and great value – much of which may be directly monetisable. Little wonder, then, that companies now look at the data that they own as one of their biggest assets. In fact, some of the giant global corporations are able to provide free services only because of the value of the data that they collect in the process (some may even uncharitably say that they provide free services only in order to garner valuable data).

With new sensors, machine-to-machine connectivity and analytics, the so-called Internet of Things (IoT) is already here and beginning to be deployed in industry, as part of the evolution to Industry 4.0. IoT will mean millions of connected devices, with massive data generation. The true value of this comes from its analysis and consequent – sometimes real-time – action, but the foundation or raw material is the basic data itself.

The advent and development of artificial intelligence (AI) platforms has made data even more invaluable. For, it is only through actual data that the algorithms for AI can be developed, refined and validated. Thus, the very development of AI requires very large amounts of data, and organisations (or countries) that own more data may well be better placed to lead the field in AI.

It is for these reasons that data has become a commodity of great value in today's world. As India increases the extent of digitalisation, data will be generated in even greater quantity and will also become more invaluable. New apps, based on data used for machine learning and AI, will add further value to data.

All this has raised a host of questions with regard to data. Broadly, they can be classified into six categories, as below:

- **Data collection**: Should there be any regulation regarding the type, extent and purpose of data collection? Will the data provider have a choice as to what to divulge and will this be based on sufficient knowledge ('informed choice')?
- **Data storage**: Who can store data? What safeguards need to be laid down and how should responsibility be specified in terms of protecting the data? If there are breaches, what is the deterrent punishment and who is specifically responsible? Where should the data be stored, in terms of national boundaries, and what is the extent of extra-territorial or trans-border jurisdiction? How best can this exercised? What are the "data sovereignty" and "protection of citizen rights" issues?
- **Data processing**: Are restrictions or limitations necessary, with regard to permissible processing, location (country) of processing, transfer of data for processing, anonymization requirements, relative responsibilities of processor and of collector?
- **Category of data**: What are the appropriate data categories: personal, sensitive, strategic, non-personal, community, etc? How is each defined? Will the definition change with context? With time? What will be the regulations for each?

- o **Data ownership**: Who is the ultimate owner of the data? If personal data is owned by the individual concerned, will s/he be paid each time it is monetized? Who owns the information that comes from analysis and value-additions to the basic data? Can the State claim rights over the data about its citizens or about its resources?
- o **Regulatory mechanisms**: What kind of regulatory mechanism/s may be needed? Should there be a single regulator for all data or is it better to regulate by sector/data type (e.g., health data, financial data, etc.)?What powers should the regulator have? Should it be a multi-stake-holder body (including business and civil society) or a government) entity?

These are but a few of the many issues and questions in this complex, rapidly-changing and extremely important domain. These require deep investigation, much thought and deliberation rather than knee-jerk, event-triggered action.

It is this overall context that a book like this, which looks at the issues with a broad and overall perspective, is of great importance and immediate relevance. One has also to look at the matter not in isolation or just in techno-economic terms, but within the overall global scenario, including the geo-political implications. This international context has to be examined and understood: the European data protection regulation, GDPR; the jousting between the US and Chinese viewpoints; the power of a few very large companies; the pro-competition rulings – and consequent fines on some companies – in Europe; the trans-border taxation issues, etc.

In India, there are vigorous on-going debates regarding privacy, protection and localisation of data. A government-appointed committee (headed by Justice Srikrishna) prepared draft legislation sometime back. More recently, another committee (led by Kris Gopalkrishnan) is working on regulations for non-personal data.

Within industry, there are varying views on these issues (particularly on data localisation). Civil society organisations too have been active with regard to privacy and rights of the individual. Academia has looked at the ramifications of any curbs on data flow and also at the consequences of a global "digital tax".

This book has covered most of these issues and provided the background on them. It has included both, global regulations (like GDPR, mentioned earlier) and the Indian context. It also has responses and views from industry, adding a unique and very useful perspective. It is a welcome addition to the limited literature in this area in India. All those interested, involved or affected by developments in this field – government, academia, civil society and industry, and also individuals – would do well to read this book. It will certainly serve to further the debate in this area and hopefully help us to reach a consensus on most issues.

Kiran Karnik is an author, independent public policy and strategy analyst, and a former President of NASSCOM. He has been involved with issues related to data privacy, data protection and data/cyber security, and is currently Honorary Chair of CII's National Committee on Telecom and Broadband.

PREFACE

The European Union new data protection law-General Data Protection Regulation (GDPR), implemented last year on 25 May'2018- has been a landmark development, in data privacy. It fundamentally changes the way data is handled by organizations. In India too, there have been significant developments on this front. A committee headed by Justice Srikrishna, has submitted the 'Personal Data Protection Bill' in July, 2018 to the government for enactment. The government has invited public comments, and the bill is likely to get introduced in parliament for enactment, in near future. The Supreme Court has passed a judgment declaring the right to privacy as a fundamental right and as an integral part of the right to life and liberty.

The impending legislation and its consequences for non-compliance of provisions has triggered an intense debate and interest not only in the general public but also in various organizations which are revisiting processes and undertaking gap assessments.

The proposed 'Personal Data Protection Bill' provides people extensive data protection rights. It stipulates significant obligations on organizations accompanied with severe penalties and compensations, in case of any data breach or harm to individuals. This can expose various organizations processing such information to significant financial and business continuity risks, in case of non-compliance.

Although much of the information on this subject is available in the public domain, the aim of this book is to share key insights and provisions in a simplified form for general awareness, which could serve as a self-assessment and implementation guide across industries, in particular the Micro/Small & Medium Enterprises (M/SME) segment, as many lack mature organizational structure and processes for such compliances.

Key highlight of this book is the industry perspective of the compliance expectations and challenges. CEOs and industry leaders from various consulting organizations and sectors- Banking, Financial services, Health and Education- have contributed to this effort, by sharing their views on various provisions of the bill and challenges expected in compliance.

We have structured this book in four sections, broadly covering - (I) Evolving Privacy Risks in a Digital World, (II) Global Data Privacy Frameworks and India's Personal Data Protection Bill, (III) Governance & Privacy Implementation and (IV) Industry Perspective.

Section I covers various developments happening on the digital front and how Social Media, Mobility, Analytics and Cloud technologies are catalyzing digital revolution thereby causing major disruptions in business models across sectors. It also highlights how emerging technologies such as IoT, Big Data, Virtual Reality and Artificial Intelligence (AI), are posing new threats and vulnerabilities to data privacy. Data is the new currency and is now used extensively for profiling through various data mining & analytical techniques. While the abundance of personal data being created offers great benefits to organizations and individuals, it is increasing the privacy risks faced by individuals. There have been rampant incidents of data security breaches compromising sensitive personal data of millions of users. As organizations transform to become digital enterprises and face increasing security and data privacy risks, creating digital trust is becoming critical for organizations to survive.

Section II covers details about the concept of privacy, various types of privacy and terms used in data privacy regulations. It provides a high level of view of the global data privacy frameworks and major regulations across countries including FIPPS, HIPPA, OECD guidelines, APEC privacy framework, EU directive 95/46/EC and GDPR, which have contributed to the prevailing data privacy laws.

The section runs through India's journey in this area, covering extant provisions of the Information Technology Act, RBI & TRAI guidelines, relating to handling of sensitive personal data and confidentiality of customer information. It further covers the general understanding of provisions of the India data privacy bill relating to data protection obligations, lawful grounds for processing, rights of the individuals, transparency & accountability requirements, cross border data transfers, data protection authority & appellate process and various penalties provisions.

Section III covers the governance & implementation framework. Privacy is a key risk; data breaches expose organizations to significant reputational and operational damage, and legal action by affected individuals.

Organizations must be put in place appropriate governance & privacy framework, to ensure compliance and should undertake data mapping and gap assessments to do risk analysis.

The implementation requirements cover various obligations that the organizations must comply - training & awareness of employees, privacy notices, data protection officer (DPO), data privacy impact risk assessments (DPIAs), data audits, adoption of security safeguards including ISO/IEC 27001 & deployment of various privacy enhancing technologies.

In section IV we bring to you, the industry perspective on data privacy and new data protection bill and the specific challenges that various industry leaders foresee in its implementation.

We have collated this feedback, through a structured questionnaire, from CEOs and industry leaders of various sectors - consulting organizations, banking, mutual fund, NBFCs, health and education. The questionnaire sought feedback on various provisions of the bill, and challenges foreseen in its implementation and in particular for MSME/SME sector. It further sought feedback on the costs involved in implementation, current data protection measures deployed by the organizations, business process changes and additional measures in terms of technology & tools that are required to meet compliance of new provisions. The section covers a summary of the feedback along with individual responses of all the respondents.

We thank Kiran Karnik, renowned author and former President of NASSCOM, for writing a foreword to this book and setting a context. We also thank Marshal Correia, erstwhile VP of HP Enterprise Services and MD, DXC Technology, for going through the book contents and writing a review.

Aravamudhan Srinivasan (DXC Technology), Nikki Ahuja (Deloitte India) and Neha Verma (Bank of Ireland), extended great help in personal capacities, in reviewing and editing this book.

We hope the book shall help in creating awareness and shall guide the organizations in particular SME/MSMEs, in complying with provisions and undertaking privacy implementations.

Prof. RK Dubey   Ajay Kr Verma

CONTENTS

SECTION I

1. Digital Revolution — 1
2. Data Privacy Risk — 9

SECTION II

3. Privacy Defined — 15
4. Global Data Privacy Frameworks - FIPPs, OECD Guidelines, APEC Framework, HIPPA, EU Directives, GDPR — 21
5. India Privacy Regulations – IT ACT, RBI, TRAI — 40
6. Personal Data Protection Bill – An Overview — 47

SECTION III

7. Implementation and Compliance Approach — 70
8. Privacy Management Framework — 73
9. Data Mapping and Gap Analysis — 82
10. Key Steps - Privacy Implementation — 93
    - 10.1 Training
    - 10.2 Privacy Notification
    - 10.3 Data Protection Officer
    - 10.4 Data Protection Impact Assessment
    - 10.5 Data Audit
    - 10.6 Security Safeguards
    - 10.7 Privacy Enhancing Technologies

SECTION IV

11	Industry Perspective – Data Privacy and Protection	134

11.1 Som Mittal, Former President and Chairman, NASSCOM

11.2 R SubramaniaKumar, Ex-CMD, Indian Overseas Bank

11.3 Rajneesh Kumar- CEO, Canara Robeco Mutual Fund

11.4 Dr Vinay Aggarwal, Chairman & MD, Pushpanjanli Crosslay Hospital

11.5 Eric Anklesaria, Global Leader -Banking & Capital markets Transformation, Capgemini

11.6 Gursharan Rai Bansal, Chief Sales & Marketing Officer, India Post Payments Bank

11.7 Smt. P V Bharathi, Managing Director & CEO, Corporation Bank

11.8 Anuj Mathur, Managing Director & CEO, Canara HSBC Life

11.9 DS Tripathi, MD & CEO, Aadhaar Housing Finance Ltd.

Annexure 1 – Glossary of Terms	179
Annexure 2 – Personal Data Protection Bill Sections and Provisions	182
Annexure 3 – ISO 27001 Ann A: Controls	188
Annexure 4 - Bibliography	189
Book Review - Marshal Correia, erstwhile VP, HP Enterprise Services and MD, DXC Technologies	191
About Authors	192

1. Digital Revolution

We are living in a digital world. Everything is going digital - be it work, education, entertainment, conversation and even relationships. There is an easy access to information and all is available on touch of a screen. It is changing the way people work, consume and communicate. Throughout the day we are online - staying connected and communicating with people, browsing or buying products and services. Every minute, we are creating a footprint in the digital world through our posts, likes, and messages. WhatsApp, Facebook, Instagram accounts and email addresses have become our virtual identities and we are all the 'digital citizens' in this virtual world.

There are around 3.9 billion people connected online today, as per the International Telecommunication Union (ITU). Internet proliferation is boosted by a combination of various factors - increasing network coverage, data affordability, rising income levels and availability of online services and content. Mobile, web, and social media are transforming customer digital experience and creating disruptions across industries. Millennials, - the new generation of people are key drivers of this change. They are tech savvy and have a marked preference for online services delivered in innovative ways. This is changing the fundamental ways of how organizations do business. Emerging technologies such as Artificial Intelligence and the Internet of Things (IoT) are bringing further disruptions in business models.

Companies such as Amazon, Uber, Alibaba, Facebook, Airbnb, WhatsApp, have already created major disruptions across sectors - Transport, Retailing, Hospitality, and Telecommunications. These companies have digital business models and are asset light. They are aggregators who own no inventories and have disrupted markets, to become billion-dollar companies in a short span of time. For example, Uber owns zero fleet but operates over millions of cars and has a valuation of over USD 62 billion; Airbnb, which has zero inventory of rooms, has over 4 million listings worldwide and is valued at USD 30 billion; Alibaba with zero manufacturing, is a storefront of more than a million products and has crossed more than USD 500 billion valuation mark; WhatsApp has over 1.5 billion active users today which Facebook bought for over USD 19 billion.

This digital revolution is already being dubbed as the fourth industrial revolution. World Economic Forum (WEF) says that there are three compelling reasons for calling it the next revolution – velocity, scope of change and systems impact.

Digital revolution is impacting industries at breakneck speed, for example - while it took telecom companies 20 years to reach 20 billion messages a day, WhatsApp reached 34 billion messages a day in less than 7 years. Uber founded in 2009, today commands 85% of the private cab business in the USA. Airbnb which was set up in 2007 now has over 4 million property listings, and operates in 65,000 cities across 190 countries. Amazon founded in 1994 as an online bookstore is now the largest internet company by revenue and market capitalization. It has a market share of 49% of the e-retail in the USA with over 300 million users. Facebook, created in 2004 has over 2 billion monthly active users (MAU) globally.

These digital disruptors can sign up millions of users overnight. The scope of impact is across industries and is also affecting entire systems of production, management and governance.

1.1 Data is the new currency

The biggest asset of these companies is data, which they are monetizing through technology to create disruptions and new revenue streams. Data is the new currency in the digital world. Exponential growth of consumer data is driving these organizations to use technology to offer a more compelling, customized and an immersive experience that creates greater loyalty and satisfaction.

Companies selling products and services need to know their customers' preferences, lifestyles, priorities and financial means. They need to analyze their historical and current purchases and understand spending patterns, interests and preferences. How people spend and the motivation behind is critical for a deeper customer insight. Artificial Intelligence & data analytics enable companies and brands to analyze data and create unique and customized consumer experiences.

Companies such as Amazon, Uber, Airbnb, and Netflix are focused on how to make the experience as convenient as possible for their customers. It is about knowing what their customers want and giving it to them when they want it. They are also looking at pushing boundaries by creating instant gratification driven by personalization and loyalty.

Amazon uses its recommendation engine as a targeted marketing tool based on historical purchases, browsing behavior, and aggregate receipt data. It uses these data insights to improve the customer experience by offering relevant items at the right time on the right page. Amazon generates almost 35% of its revenue through its recommendation engine. The ability to leverage customer insights is the secret to its customer loyalty. Amazon reported that 44% of US households were part of their Amazon Prime loyalty program and they spend about USD 2,500 a year which is almost six times more than what its non-Prime members spend.

1.2 Technologies driving Digital Revolution

Internet connectivity along with Social, Mobile, Analytics and Cloud also known as SMAC technologies have been the foundation for digital innovation. Emerging technologies such as IoT, Big Data, Virtual Reality and Artificial Intelligence are further speeding up the digital transformation. Convergence of all these technologies gives rise to next generation applications and new business opportunities.

The explosive growth of social media - WhatsApp, Facebook, YouTube and other platforms has increased digital access to a huge segment of the population. Almost a quarter of the world's population is now on Facebook. In the US, 80% of internet users are on this platform. People spend an average of 2 hours and 15 minutes on social media each day, which is almost one third of the time spent online. This shows the tremendous power of social media in increasing the reach to consumers. Apart from social messaging, these platforms have shifted the power in the hands of masses to influence any issues – be it political, social, ethical or even commerce. Organizations see the importance of using social media to connect with customers and generate insights, stimulate demand, and create targeted product offerings.

The increasing penetration of smart phones is further speeding up this growth. As per the CISCO white paper- 'Forecast and Trends: 2017–2022', the smart phones network traffic will outpace personal computers (PCs) in near future. Smart phones will account for 44% of total IP traffic by 2022, up from 18 percent in 2017. As per a BCG report, the number of mobile internet users may reach up to 3 billion by 2020. Smart phones today have capabilities such as enhanced processors, high capacity storage memories, near field communication (NFC), and high resolution cameras. They are no longer only communication devices, but have transformed to become commerce enablers.

Emergence of smart phones has enabled development of new payment technologies viz. mobile banking, Unstructured Supplementary Service Data (USSD) - which facilitates online transactions even without internet connectivity, contactless payments using NFC features, secure online banking through OTP (onetime password) on mobile phones - which serves as dual authentication including finger print validations.

Big Data Analytics and Cloud are helping organizations process large volumes of data. Cloud computing has reduced the cost of storage, making it affordable to store large volumes of data and reduced the cost of computing power.

Internet of things (IoT) along with advancements in Artificial Intelligence (AI) is bringing a technology revolution leading to greater automation and development of autonomous & intelligent systems that have near human capabilities. IoT is an ecosystem of connected smart devices that interact with each other and with individuals, collecting all kinds of data. This is exploding from 2 billion devices in 2006 to a projected 200 billion by 2020. It is a primary driver for our data vaults exploding. Artificial Intelligence (AI) refers to technologies capable of performing tasks requiring human intelligence. AI is also behind the chatbot revolution, making personal assistants such as Siri and Alexa that can think and converse more like humans.

1.3 Digital Revolution powering innovation

Extensive and innovative uses of personal data are bringing tremendous economic and social benefits. It is creating opportunities for process improvements, gains in productivity, cost reductions apart from realizing higher uptime & availability through predictive maintenance, improving customer service and making systems agile for quicker decision making.

There are estimated economic gains of USD 10-15 trillion in global GDP over the next 2 decades, with savings of trillions of dollars through cost reductions and improved services. We are seeing great innovations such as development of autonomous vehicles, automated warehouses using robotic applications for delivery, smart cities with auto-control lighting systems, remote security systems with auto feeds from CCTV cameras deployed across the cities, and automated parking systems and smart energy grids. Automations in agriculture range from seed sowing to spraying of insecticides, harvesting of crops, sampling and grading of produce, image analysis of satellite data for improving crop yields and analyzing cropping patterns are a few other examples. Smart healthcare systems use wearables & sensors to monitor health parameters, transmit data from remote locations to hospitals & doctors, for medical dispensation and help in preventive & critical care. These developments in Artificial Intelligence & Deep Learning besides augmenting human capabilities are helping in predictive risk analysis, pricing and making automated decisions.

1.4 Exponential Growth of data & risk

The amount of data we produce today is mind-boggling. There is an enormous amount of activity on Internet - social media, mails, texts, digital photographs, services and the internet of things. In one of the publications by Jacobs Media, – "What Happens in An Internet Minute" by Lori Lewis, social media guru, the results for 2018 are breathtaking. In one minute, people exchange*d* 18 million text messages, shared 38 million WhatsApp messages, and sent 187 million emails. Users watched 4.3 million YouTube videos and made 3.7 million searches on the internet.

Data Protection and Privacy Implementation

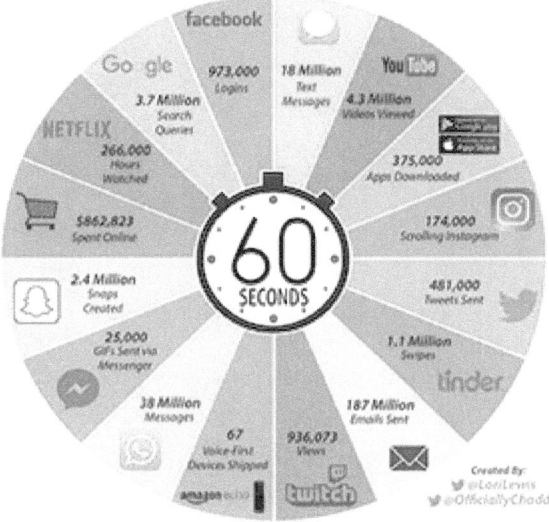

As per a study published by IBM, 90% of the data in the world today has been generated in the last 2 years. Every 2 days, we created as much data as was created until 2013. This pace is only accelerating with the growth of IoT. The data statistics are astounding- IoT devices produce 5 quintillion bytes of data every day (that's 2.5 followed by 18 zeros). This is only a beginning with the number of IoT devices growing.

Citi Bank : ePrivacy& data protection report

A large percentage of data generated is personal (i.e. it relates to specific individuals or identifiable individuals). Such data may be structured data that is stored in formal records and databases or unstructured data that has been generated on social media or other online activity. As per Merrill Lynch, 80-90% of data generated today is unstructured. The use of big data, AI, algorithms and machine learning - can help analyze such data to give it a context or relate it to an individual or segment of population.

While the abundance of personal data available offers great benefits to organizations and individuals, it is increasing the privacy risks faced by them. Securing personal data has become a greater challenge. Individuals are exposed to increased potential harms - data breaches, unauthorized data usage, identity thefts, etc. The IoT brings its own set of unique digital risks and challenges. The devices carrying sensors need to be smart enough so that they can be upgraded to protect against emerging vulnerabilities. Such devices could fail to perform on account of the interconnected subsystems and cause physical damage and or result in a data breach. The systems could be compromised on account of any failure in controls or because of hacking. All this adds to the increasing risks to digital security. Data now traverses millions of devices and systems that transcend organization, national boundaries and jurisdictions. This brings in new challenges in apportioning accountability, making privacy controls difficult for organizations to implement and regulators to regulators to enforce.

2. Data Privacy Risk

The digital world brings in new threats & vulnerabilities to data privacy. The growing value of personal data increases the risks that data can be used in ways that neither the organization nor the individual can imagine. There is an increasing risk as we have no control of our personal data and how it is being collected and used.
It is difficult for individuals to understand and make choices related to the use of their personal data, while giving consent. Individuals face either a lack of information or overly detailed information in privacy notices and find it difficult to assess information risks when confronted with complex information and competing interests.

2.1 Personal Data & Privacy Risk

People share their personal data in many ways. Data is shared with many entities for various services they wish to buy or subscribe to.

It could be a requirement in the form of Know Your Customer (KYC) information, which is a prerequisite for many services viz. banking and other financial services or could be basic personal information for billing, invoicing and delivery of a product. Sensitive information such as the passwords, bank account or card information used for purchases are stored digitally. All such sensitive data is susceptible to misuse and open to threats.

Quite often, people also share personal data on various websites where there are no direct purchases but for some perceived benefits such as information sharing or enhanced experience. People almost accept this and part with personal information to gain free access to such sites and applications. People also share & post a lot of personal information, photographs etc. across various social media platforms.

Apart from the direct data collection, a lot of data is also gathered and collated through indirect means. This could be data collected from social websites or the individual's purchase and browsing history, using cookies. Cookie is a small program sent from a website and installed on the user's computer or device and is used to collect or to record a user's activity. There could be 'tracking cookies' used to record browsing history of individuals or 'authentication cookies' used to remember individuals' credentials and to know their login status. Data is also collected through various sensors in personal devices, wearables and smart phones. Various mobile apps track user location data and other information, for which permission is sought while downloading those apps. Users are unaware of the risks associated with such permissions to access their data and unwittingly grant such permissions.

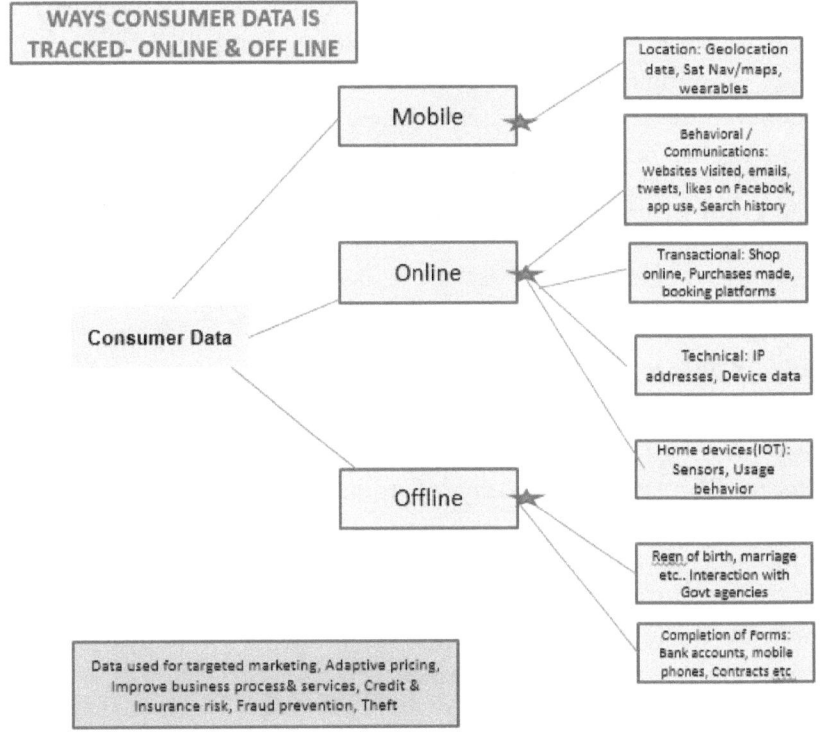

Source: Citi Research

All such data is used for profiling through various data mining and analytical techniques. Such profiling could be used to send targeted messages and advertisements to influence purchase decisions. This may contravene basic privacy principals of data collection, purpose limitation and transparency.

The combination of various methods of collecting and processing data allows for a more detailed monitoring of individual's activities. Increased attention is needed to mitigate the privacy risks to individuals posed by monitoring, unanticipated secondary usage, and data security breaches.

All such data shared by an individual is exposed to digital security risks from the point of confidentiality, integrity and availability, besides violating data privacy principles. There have been various incidents of data security breaches where sensitive personal data of individuals has been compromised.

2.2 Data Privacy Violations & Impact

Every day we hear of security incidents and breaches. Spam, phishing attacks, malware and virus attacks are something that everyone has encountered. There are campaigns run by the government and various regulatory agencies such as Reserve Bank of India (RBI), Telecom Regulatory Authority of India (TRAI), Banks and other institutions to create awareness among users against these risks.

Major data breaches have been reported from even the best of organizations such as Google, Facebook, e-bay and many others, suggesting that our data is not safe.

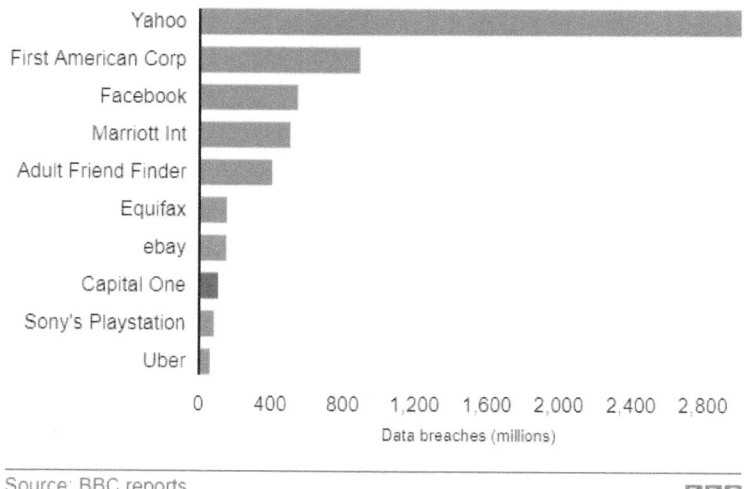

In one of the largest data breaches reported - consultancy firm Cambridge Analytica used data of around 87 million Facebook accounts to profile voters and use in the US 2016 election campaign. It was found that Facebook processed the personal information of users unfairly by giving app developers access to their information without proper consent. Cambridge Analytica had to shut down operations after suffering a sharp drop in business because of adverse publicity and mounting litigations, on account of the misuse of personal data and it had to file for bankruptcy proceedings.

Facebook reported a data breach wherein cyber attackers stole data from around 29 million Facebook accounts using an automated program. Hackers used vulnerability in the 'View As' functionality in Facebook, which allowed users to see what their own profile looks like to someone else.

Personal details of about 106 million individuals across the US and Canada were stolen in a hack targeting financial services firm Capital One, recently.

Yahoo, earlier reported a breach impacting more than a billion accounts. In addition, individual names, dates of birth and email addresses, sensitive data such as passwords, security questions and answers were also compromised.

There have been many other breaches reported and even larger number breaches that go unreported. While, the risk to individuals is high where sensitive data such as passwords, bank accounts or credit card data etc. are stolen, these incidents have huge implications for organizations too, in terms of negative publicity, actions from regulatory authorities across the countries, erosion of shareholder value, punitive damages and enormous litigation costs.

2.3 Building Digital Trust

As organizations transform to become digital enterprises and are exposed to increasing security and data privacy risks, establishing digital trust is critical and organizations need to address three primary areas - People, Processes and Technology, to build this trust.

People - People are at the heart of digital trust. No matter the state of art technology used by an organization, it is the people that make the difference in terms of how it is implemented or used. Compliance of security measures to a large extent depends on people. Organizations need to invest in training and creating awareness among staff about digital security and privacy. It is critical to have the right skill-set and leadership for any digital transformation and have clear role definitions and accountability, for compliance with security policies and procedures.

Process - Digital trust is a measure of consumer confidence in an organization's ability to protect and secure data and privacy of individuals. Apart from various information security measures, compliance with data protection principles and laws is critical to create assurance and trust. Organizations need to improve data governance and create transparency in the use and storage of data. They must focus on data privacy risk assessments and data audits to meet the emerging compliance requirements.

Technology - Organizations must ensure that enterprise systems are reliable, secure and trusted. System availability is very critical in the digital world, and any outages or compromise of systems can seriously hamper user's access and impact trust. Organizations must embed privacy and security during new product development or technology deployment and ensure that the deployment of new technologies such as IoT, AI, etc have sufficient safeguards built in before deployment. Organizations must keep abreast of emerging risks in these areas.

3. Privacy Defined

People generally attach different meanings to the word privacy – embarrassment, isolation, intimacy, confidentiality or secrecy. Privacy, however, is more than just hiding something or keeping it secret. It is, in essence, the right to be left alone. In other words, it is the ability or entitlement of an individual to seclude oneself and selectively share personal information.

The right to be left alone, as the basic proposition of a right to privacy, was first enunciated by Samuel Warren and Louis Brandeis in a law article published in 1890 Harvard Law Review. Since then privacy laws and constitutions of many countries have reaffirmed the right to privacy of an individual and treat it as a part of the fundamental right to life and liberty.

Privacy - A Fundamental Right

In most countries, the Right to Privacy is treated as a fundamental right. In the US, the constitutional provisions of 'Fourth Amendment' form the basis of the "right to privacy," i.e. the right to be left alone. It considers an enjoyment of personal privacy as fundamental to a free and civil society.

In Europe, the protection of natural persons in relation to the processing of personal data is a fundamental right. Article 8 of the European Convention on Human Rights (an international treaty to protect human rights and fundamental freedoms in Europe) stipulates that everyone has the right to respect for his private and family life, his home and his correspondence.

In India too, Supreme Court in its landmark judgment in the case - Justice K.S Puttaswamy (Retd.) v. Union of India and Others, upheld privacy to be a fundamental right under the Constitution of India. It proclaimed that right to privacy is protected as an intrinsic part of the right to life and personal liberty under Article 21 and as a part of the freedoms guaranteed by Part III of the Constitution. The Judgment acknowledges that privacy allows each individual to be left alone. The right to privacy is an inalienable right to protect the individual from unwanted intrusion into their private life, including sexuality, religion, political affiliation, etc. The judgment recognizes that privacy is intrinsic to other liberties guaranteed as fundamental rights under the Constitution. It is an element of human dignity, and ensures that a human being can lead a life of dignity by, among other things, exercising a right to make essential choices, to express oneself, to dissent, etc.

3.1 Types of Privacy

What is considered private may differ among cultures and individuals. Different cultures and nations have varied outlooks about privacy or what constitutes an invasion of privacy. Privacy pertaining to individuals may relate to personal privacy or informational privacy.

Personal Privacy

Personal privacy could relate to 'bodily privacy' - privacy in relation to the exposure of their body to others or 'spatial privacy'- privacy of space, such as family life and intimate relations.

People may like to preserve their privacy through covering their bodies with clothes or seeking seclusion. Physical privacy is about preventing any intrusions in to one's physical space. Trespass, Stalking and Voyeurism are considered a crime in all societies. Most nations guarantee rights to individuals against any unauthorized searches of their bodies and possessions.

Informational Privacy

Informational or data privacy is about ownership rights to information about individuals, how such information can be collected, processed, stored or shared by anyone. Individuals have rights to personal identifiable information about themselves and may object to any information such as their religion, sexual orientation, political affiliation, or personal activities, from being revealed to avoid any discrimination, embarrassment, or damage to their personal/professional reputations.

Information privacy may relate to:

a. **Financial Privacy** - This is about safeguarding a person's financial transactions or privacy about financial relationships, to avoid any fraud or identity thefts.

b. **Internet Privacy** - This may include concerns about who has access to one's information shared on internet, emails, social messaging platforms - Facebook, WhatsApp, Instagram etc., and for what purposes one's information may be used.

c. **Medical Privacy** - This is about protecting information about an individual's health, medical conditions or records and even sexual preferences. Sharing of such information could result in embarrassment and affect his or her insurance coverage or employment.

d. **Political & Religious Beliefs** - Sharing of such information could result in discrimination of an individual and hamper his or her freedom to exercise one's beliefs and Choices. Ethnicity, Caste or Racial Information - This could result in discrimination or exploitation.

3.2 Data Privacy Terms

It is important to understand a few key terms that are used in the context of data privacy referred to in data privacy regulations. For the purpose of understanding, we have taken reference to the meaning of these terms as defined in European Union General Data Protection Regulation (GDPR) and in India's Personal Data Protection Bill;

a. Data Controller or Data Fiduciary

In GDPR, 'Data Controller' is anyone who determines the purposes and means of processing personal data.

India's Personal Data protection bill uses the term "Data Fiduciary" for such entity. Data Fiduciary means 'any person, including the state, a company, any juristic entity or individual who alone or in conjunction with others determines the purpose and means of processing of personal data'.

b. Data Processor

A Data Processor is anyone who is responsible for processing personal data on behalf of a Data controller (Fiduciary). Per the India Personal Data Protection Bill it means 'any person, including the State, a company, any juristic entity or any individual who processes personal data on behalf of a data fiduciary, but does not include an employee of the data fiduciary'.

c. Data Subject or Data Principal

In GDPR, 'Data Subject' is an identified or identifiable natural person.

India's Personal Data Protection Bill uses the term 'Data Principal' for such a person. 'Data Principal means a natural person who is directly or indirectly identifiable, having regard to any characteristic, trait, attribute or any other feature of the identity of such a natural person, or any combination of such features, or any combination of such features with any other information'.

d. Personal Data

Personal data means 'data about or relating to a natural person who is directly or indirectly identifiable, having regard to any characteristic, trait, attribute or any other feature of the identity of such a natural person, or any combination of such features, or any combination of such features with any other information'.

There is no exhaustive list of identifiers given in the Personal Data Protection Bill, but going by the general understanding as given in GDPR, such identifiers cover:

Direct Identifiers include name and address of an individual, identification number such as Aadhaar or PAN, telephone or mobile number, e-mail address, or biometric information.

In-direct Identifiers include attributes that can be combined with other information to identify an individual. It includes gender, date of birth, geo-location data, place of birth, religion, employment information, medical information, educational details, and financial information.

Online Identifiers could be devices, applications, tools and protocols, such as internet protocol addresses, cookie identifiers or other identifiers such as radio frequency identification tags, etc.

Sensitive Personal Data: Sensitive Personal Data is information which is sensitive and its processing could create a significant risk to the fundamental rights and freedoms of an individual. Personal Data Protection Bill lists following data as sensitive:

- passwords
- financial data
- health data
- official identifier
- sex life
- sexual orientation
- biometric data
- genetic data
- transgender status
- intersex status
- caste or tribe, or Religious or political belief or affiliation.

4. Global Data Privacy Frameworks

Privacy concerns emerged in the late 1960s with the post-industrial information revolution and the increasing use of personal data processing. While the advantages of using computers for more efficient data processing were evident, there were growing concerns on the potential misuse of personal data and its impact on human rights.

This led to formation of task forces and commissions in various countries to study the privacy issues and its impact. The concerns identified in these studies and reports contributed to legislative responses in several countries notably – The U.S. Freedom of Information Act (1966), the Fair Credit Reporting Act (1970) and the Privacy Act (1974), the Swedish enactment of a data protection legislation and setting up of Data Inspection Board in 1973, the Canadian Human Rights Act (1977), the Netherlands Act on Personal Data Registrations and the creation of the Data Protection Authority (1988), the French Law on Informatics and Freedom (1978).

Many other countries across Europe and members of Organization for Economic Co-operation and Development (OECD) adopted national legislations on data privacy by 1980. Countries adopted various approaches to data privacy. Most of the countries adopted national legislations, laying down guidelines for protecting data privacy and its enforcement framework. Few countries such as the US have adopted sector specific legislations in the areas of financial services, healthcare, and credit reporting, besides consumer protection regulations to safeguard privacy.

In addition to legislative actions, many countries such as the US and Japan encourage and support self-regulation through self-regulatory policies and model industry codes. Organizations are encouraged to adopt and get certified against industry codes and standards that help create assurance and greater acceptance by various stakeholders.

In the following sections, we will run through a few of the global initiatives on data privacy which have been implemented over a period of the last few decades and have evolved keeping pace with the technological changes and emerging needs for cross border data flows.

4.1 FIPPs

The Fair Information Practice Principles (FIPPs) formulated by the United States Federal State Commission, are a set of internationally recognized principles that govern information privacy policies and practices in an electronic marketplace. These core elements have evolved since 1973, when these were proposed by the US Advisory Committee on Automated Personal Data Systems and are incorporated in data privacy laws, policies and governance documents around the world.

The FIPP are only recommendatory in nature and adopted by organizations as a part of self-regulation. These principles, however, form the basis of many laws at federal & state level viz. Privacy Act, Fair Credit Reporting Act, the Electronic Communications Privacy Act, Video Privacy Protection Act and Cable TV Protection and Competition Act, in the US.

The core principles of FIPP are as under:

a) **Notice/ Awareness** - The Notice principle is the most fundamental of the fair information practice principles. Organizations are required to provide consumers clear and conspicuous notice of information practices that these organizations follow, before any personal information is collected. It includes identification of the entity collecting the data, what information they collect, how they collect it, how they use it, whether any information collected is disclosed to other entities and the steps taken by the data collector to ensure confidentiality, integrity and quality of the data.

b) **Choice/ Consent** - The Choice principle relates to giving consumers options as to how any personal information that organizations collect may be used. Data collectors must afford consumers an opportunity to consent to secondary uses of their personal information including for any advertising purpose or transfer of personal information, to entities other than the data collector. This should be facilitated through a process of 'Opt-in' or 'Opt-out', to record customer consent.

c) **Access/ Participation** - This principle seeks to provide individuals access to data about themselves i.e., to view the data that an entity holds and seek data accuracy and completeness. Access is essential to improve accuracy of the data collected. This benefits both data collectors, who rely on such data, and consumers who might otherwise be harmed by adverse decisions based on incorrect data.

d) **Integrity/ Security** - Security refers to a data collector's obligation to protect personal information against any unauthorized access, use or disclosure and against loss or destruction. Data collectors must ensure that the data they collect is accurate and secure. This involves both managerial and technical measures to provide such protections.

e) **Enforcement of FIPP** - The Federal Trade Commission (FTC) seeks enforcement through self-regulation by the data collectors. Efforts to encourage self-regulation are based on the belief that greater protection of personal privacy will benefit businesses as well as consumers, by increasing consumer confidence and participation in the online marketplace. The key enforcement mechanisms to emerge in self-regulatory efforts are the privacy seal programs such as the TRUSTe, BBBOnLine Privacy, CPA WebTrust etc. Websites that carry these privacy seals, create confidence amongst users about adequacy of security compliance by such websites.

Individuals also have the right to initiate a civil action for any misuse of information or for any other harm caused. Besides, any violations can attract civil and criminal penalties levied by the government.

4.2 OECD GUIDELINES

The Organization for Economic Co-operation and Development (OECD) is a multilateral body which was setup in 1960, when 18 European countries along with United States and Canada joined together to create a forum to address the economic, social and environmental challenges of globalization. Today, it has 36 Member countries.

The privacy guidelines adopted by OECD in 1980 represent the first internationally agreed-upon set of privacy principles. They have influenced the development of national data protection legislation and model codes not only within the OECD member countries but across regions.

The OECD privacy guidelines were a response to emerging concerns about the possible impact on the rights of individuals resulting from the increasing automated processing of personal information. It was also the recognition of importance of personal data flows in the growing global economy and likely adverse impact of restrictions, placed by different privacy legislations across countries, on global trade.

The Privacy guidelines have been framed in a concise and technologically neutral language and prescribed as minimum standards which the member countries should adopt while endeavoring not to create any unjustified obstacles to trans-border flows of personal data. In 2007, the OECD Council further adopted a recommendation on cross-border co-operation in the enforcement of laws protecting privacy.

The privacy guidelines have been embodied in 'eight basic principles' that the member nations must endeavor to adhere to:

a) **Collection Limitation Principle** - There should be limits to the collection of personal data and any such data should be obtained by lawful and fair means and, where appropriate, with the knowledge or consent of the data subject.

b) **Data Quality Principle** - Personal data should be relevant to the purposes for which they are to be used and, to the extent necessary for those purposes, should be accurate, complete and kept up-to-date.

c) **Purpose Specification Principle** - The purposes for which personal data are collected should be specified no later than the time of data collection and subsequent use should be limited to the fulfillment of those purposes.

d) **Use Limitation Principle** - Personal data should not be disclosed, made available or otherwise used for purposes other than those specified.

e) **Security Safeguards Principle** - Personal data should be protected by reasonable security safeguards against risks such as loss or unauthorized access, destruction, use, modification or disclosure of data.

f) **Openness Principle** - There should be a general policy of openness about developments, practices and policies with respect to personal data. Means should be readily available of establishing the existence and nature of personal data, and the main purposes of their use, as well as the identity and usual residence of the data controller.

g) **Individual Participation Principle** - An individual should have the right to obtain from a data controller, confirmation of whether the data controller has data relating to him/ her and to have communicated the same to him/ her within a reasonable time and manner.

h) **Accountability Principle** - A data controller should be accountable for complying with measures which give effect to the principles stated above.

These guidelines have influenced the development of privacy legislations across OECD member countries and beyond. The implementation initiatives included legislation, self-regulation, and enforcement measures empowering individuals to exercise rights, and punitive compensations for compliance failures.

4.3 Asia-Pacific Economic Cooperation (APEC) Privacy Framework

APEC is a multi-national organization with a mandate to encourage economic growth, cooperation, trade and investment in the Asia-Pacific region. Seven of the 21 APEC countries are also OECD members. OECD guidelines were instrumental in the development of the Asia-Pacific Economic Cooperation (APEC) Privacy Framework.

APEC countries agreed on a framework aimed at development of appropriate information privacy protections and ensuring the free flow of information in the Asia-Pacific region which is vital to promote electronic commerce and trade. The framework was adopted in 2005 and later updated in 2015.

In addition to other similarities between APEC and OECD principles, the APEC Framework also is a non-binding instrument. Key initiatives launched as a part of the framework were:

    a. **Cross Border Privacy Rules (CBPR)** - The Cross-Border Privacy Rules were endorsed by APEC to facilitate personal information flows among APEC economies. It lays down criteria for bodies to become recognized accountability agents. It also prescribes a process for information controllers to be certified as CBPR system compliant, by a recognized accountability agent, basis a set of defined assessment criteria.

    b. **Privacy Recognition for Processors System (PRP)** - The PRP system represents the baseline criteria, an information processor must meet in order to be compliant and certified by an APEC recognized accountability agent. This provides assurance with respect to the processor's privacy policies and practices.

    c. **Cross-Border Privacy Enforcement Arrangement (CPEA)** - The CPEA is a multilateral arrangement to facilitate cooperation and information sharing amongst Privacy Enforcement Authorities in the APEC region for better cross-border privacy enforcement. The Privacy enforcement authorities have powers to conduct investigations and/ or pursue enforcement proceedings. The arrangement further allows corporate bodies to undertake cross border data transfers basis Binding Corporate Rules (BCR) that help ensure that privacy standards be maintained.

APEC Privacy Principles

    a. **Notice** - Personal information controllers should provide adequate notice about the information that is collected, purpose of collection and its intended use.

b. **Access and Correction** - Data subjects should be able to reasonably access their data that lies with information controllers and have their data rectified or updated.

c. **Use of Personal Information** - Use of personal information collected should be limited to the stated purposes of collection and other compatible or related purposes only.

d. **Collection Limitation** - The collection of personal information should be limited to the specific purposes of collection and its use.

e. **Choice** - Data subjects should be provided a mechanism to exercise choice in relation to the collection, use and disclosure of their personal information.

f. **Integrity of Personal Information** - Personal information should be accurate, complete and kept up-to date.

g. **Preventing Harm** - Specific obligations should be placed on Information controllers to prevent risk of harm from any misuse of information and the remedial measures should be proportionate to the likelihood and severity of the harm.

h. **Security Safeguards:** Personal information controllers should adopt suitable safeguards to protect information against any risk of harm. Such safeguards should be proportional to the likelihood and severity of the harm and sensitivity of the information.

i. **Accountability:** The information controller should be accountable for complying with the privacy principles and should exercise due diligence and take reasonable steps when personal information is to be transferred to another person or organization or in case of any cross-border transfer.

4.4 HIPAA

Healthcare Insurance Portability and Accountability Act (HIPAA) is a US federal law enacted in 1996. The original intent of HIPAA was to reduce costs, simplify administrative processes, and improve the privacy and security of individuals' health information in the healthcare industry.

Further changes and amendments were introduced through Privacy Rule of 2000, the Security Rule of 2003, the Enforcement Rule of 2006, the Health Information Technology for Economic and Clinical Health Act (HITECH), the American Recovery and Reinvestment Act (ARRA) introduced in 2009 and the Omnibus Final Rule of 2013 enacted further legislation within HIPAA.

Protected Health Information (PHI) and Covered Entities

HIPAA's Privacy Rule was enacted to protect the confidentiality of patients' health information. The Privacy Rules defined Protected Health Information (PHI) as 'any information held by a covered entity which concerns health status, the provision of healthcare, or payment for healthcare that can be linked to an individual', including demographic information (e.g., addresses, phone numbers, etc.). PHI can relate to the past, present, or future physical or mental health or condition of a patient.

These privacy rules regulate the use and disclosure of PHI by covered entities, business associates and third party service providers having or processing protected heath information. The Covered Entities (CEs) include - healthcare providers, health plan providers, and healthcare clearing houses who electronically transmit any health information. Business Associate (BA) is a person or entity that performs certain functions or activities that involve the use or disclosure of PHI on behalf of, or provides services to a CE.

Privacy rules require a CE to notify the individual of how the PHI shall be used and the circumstances under which it will be disclosed and to whom. It shall appoint a privacy officer for any grievance handling and creating awareness about privacy rules and training of its staff.

Disclosure of PHI

CE can disclose such information as under:

- Patients' information can be released without authorization if the purpose is for treatment, payment, or healthcare operations.
- Disclosure of patients' PHI for anything other than treatment, payment, or healthcare operations requires completion of an authorization.
- Certain exceptions exist for public health monitoring activities (e.g. disease reporting), government oversight, and some law enforcement investigations.
- Disclosure of PHI to any third parties for marketing activities is prohibited except with prior authorization.

Right of access to PHI

Privacy rules give an individual the right to access and obtain copies of its PHI from the provider. The PHI can be in digital format and individual shall have the right to have it in a desired format or transmitted to any third party. The individual shall further have a right to get corrections done in case of any inaccuracy. It can further request restrictions to the use or disclosure of their PHI except in cases specified.

Notice of Privacy Practices

Privacy rules require a CE to provide a notice of its privacy practices covering the uses or disclosures of the individual's information. All patients have the right to obtain and read a copy of the organization's

Notice of Privacy Practices and be informed of its rights to personal health information, provider's obligations and grievance handling mechanism.

HIPAA Security Rule

The HIPAA Security Rule requires the CEs and their business associates (BAs) to implement appropriate administrative, physical and technical safeguards to protect the confidentiality, integrity, and availability of ePHI (PHI stored, transmitted or used electronically). Security rules are focused on ePHI, given the proliferation of mobile devices and active use of Bring Your Own Device (BYOD) in organizations. Mobility brings extra risks through possibility of unauthorized access to data, loss of device, lack of encryptions and possibility of hacking through insecure channels of communication.

Covered entities and business associates must develop and implement policies and procedures to protect the security of ePHI they create, receive, maintain or transmit. Each entity must analyze the risks to ePHI in its environment and create solutions appropriate against reasonably anticipated threats. What is reasonable and appropriate depends on the nature of the entity's business, as well as its size, complexity and resources.

The Breach Notification Rule

Breach is an impermissible use or disclosure of PHI that compromises the security or privacy of PHI.

The HIPAA Breach Notification Rule requires CEs to notify the affected individuals and the Secretary of the Department of Health and Human Services, of any breach of unsecured PHI. Such notifications must be provided without unreasonable delay and no later than 60 days following the discovery of a breach. BAs of covered entities must also notify the covered entity of breaches at or by the business associate. In case of a potential breach, the onus is on the CE to prove and demonstrate that there is a low probability of ePHI being compromised, based on a risk assessment and other mitigations such as encryption, types of identifiers etc,

The data breaches can invite penalties up to USD 50,000 per day for each violation and up to USD 1.5 million per year for each category of violation. The extent of penalty depends on the nature and extent of breach, neglect in taking reasonable preventive steps and mitigations post breach detection. This is besides civil lawsuits by the affected individuals for damages incurred. Extreme cases of willful neglect could even lead to criminal proceedings.

The HIPAA Enforcement Rule

The Office of Civil Rights (OCR) has the entrusted responsibility to enforce HIPAA compliance through audits and financial penalties.

OCR is authorized to investigate complaints that have been filed. It conducts compliance reviews to determine if covered entities have implemented the appropriate security safeguards and policies as mandated by HIPAA. The OCR also issues guidance and conducts awareness and outreach programs to foster compliance.

4.5 Directive 95/46/EC

Directive 95/46/EC was a European Union directive adopted in 1995 for regulating the processing of personal data within the European Union. The European Commission realized that diverging data protection legislations amongst EU Member States impeded the free flow of data within the EU. It proposed the Data Protection Directive to harmonize data protection within the European Union and to ensure protection of individuals with regard to the processing of personal data and on the free movement of such data.

The directives contain principles for the protection of the rights and freedoms of individuals and in particular the right to privacy. The principles enunciated are on lines of those contained in the European Convention 1981 for the protection of Individuals with regard to automatic processing of personal data.

All the member states were required to bring into force the laws, regulations and administrative provisions, necessary to comply with this Directive within three years from the date of its adoption.

Supervisory Authority

Each member state is required to designate one or more public authorities that are responsible for monitoring the application of the provisions adopted by the member states, pursuant to this directive. Such authority shall have powers to investigative, collect all the information necessary for the performance of its supervisory duties and effective powers of intervention.

Working Party under Article 29

A working party was set up, having a representation of the supervisory authorities of each Member State. The role of the working party was advisory with a mandate to examine issues covering the application of national measures adopted under this directive, to contribute to the uniform application of such measures and advise the Commission on amendments for any additional or specific measures to safeguard the rights and freedoms of natural persons with regard to processing of personal data.

The General Data Protection Regulation (GDPR), adopted in April 2016, has superseded the Data Protection Directive and came in to effect on 25 May, 2018.

4.6 GDPR

In April 2016, the European Parliament adopted the GDPR, replacing its Data Protection Directive, which was enacted in 1995. The directives allowed the Member States of EU to adopt and customize the law to the needs of its citizens, which led to divergence in adoption of rules. The GDPR addresses these concerns and also the issues emerging from increasing digitization and use of automated processing of personal data. GDPR legislation is designed to harmonize data privacy laws across Europe, providing greater protection and rights to individuals and full adoption by all the member countries.

Major changes brought about in GDPR include increased territorial scope, penalties for non-compliance, strengthening provisions relating to consent, accountability, data subject rights, data breach notifications, privacy by design, appointment of data protection officer, conduct of data protection impact assessments and cross border data transfers.

General FAQs around GDPR are as under:

Where does the GDPR apply to?
GDPR applies to the processing of personal data of individuals, who are in the European Union, where the processing activities are related to offering of any goods or services or the monitoring of their behavior within the Union. This is regardless of whether the processing takes place in the Union.

So, the GDPR applies to processing carried out by organizations operating within the EU. It also applies to organizations outside the EU that offer goods or services to individuals in the EU.

What are the administrative fines & penalties in GDPR?

GDPR has introduced administrative fines, up to EUR 10 million or up to 2% of the total worldwide annual turnover of the preceding financial year, whichever is higher, for any infringements of provisions relating to - children consent or not meeting 'general obligations of processors and controllers' including data protection by design, maintaining records of processing, security of processing, data breach notifications to supervisory authority & data subjects, conduct of Data Protection Impact Assessments (DPIA) and appointment of Data Protection Officer (DPO).

There are more stringent administrative fines up to EUR 20 million, or up to 4% of the total worldwide annual turnover of the preceding financial year, whichever is higher, for serious infringements relating to data processing principles, lawful basis of processing, conditions of consent, processing of the special category of data, data subject rights and cross border data transfer provisions.

What are the principles governing GDPR?

GDPR lays down following principles that are a must for compliance and every data controller is under obligation to ensure its compliance. Principles relating to processing of personal data include:

a. **Lawfulness, Fairness & Transparency** - Personal data must be processed lawfully, fairly and transparently in relation to the data subject.

b. **Purpose Limitation** - Personal data must only be collected for specified, explicit and legitimate purposes, and not further processed in any way incompatible with them.

c. **Data Minimization** - The data should be adequate, relevant and limited to what is necessary in relation to the purposes for which they are processed.

- d. **Accuracy** - The data should be accurate and, where necessary, kept up to date, with inaccurate data erased or corrected without delay.

- e. **Storage limitation** - The data should be stored for no longer than is necessary for the purposes for which the personal data are processed except where personal data will be processed solely for archiving purposes in the public interest, scientific or historical research/ statistical purposes.

- f. **Security, Integrity & Confidentiality** - The data shall be processed in a manner that ensures appropriate security of the personal data, including protection against unauthorized or unlawful processing and against accidental loss, destruction or damage.

What is lawful processing?

Processing shall be lawful only if it is based on consent of the data subject or for fulfillment of any contractual or legal obligations or to protect any public or legitimate interests.

Consent by the individual should be for a specific purpose and explicit for any sensitive data involved. Where the age of the individual is less than 16 years, consent must be given or authorized by the holder of parental responsibility over the child.

What are the obligations of data controller under GDPR?

The data controller should be able to demonstrate compliance with all six data processing principles and implement appropriate technical and organizational measures to ensure that processing complies with GDPR's requirements and that it implements a level of security appropriate to the risk. It must maintain specific records of processing activities and compliance, besides undertaking staff awareness trainings.

What specific rights are enshrined upon data subjects under GDPR?

The GDPR provides the following rights to individuals:

a. **The rights to be informed** - Individuals have the right to be informed about the collection and use of their personal data. Privacy information incorporating details about data collected, purpose, retention period, data subject rights etc. has to be shared before or at the time data is collected.

b. **The rights of access** - Individuals have the right to access their personal data and submit Subject Access Requests (SAR) and such a request has to be responded within one month by the organization.

c. **The right to rectification** - Individuals have the right to get their data updated and rectified for any inaccuracy. Such a request has to be complied with within a month.

d. **The right to restrict processing** - Individuals have the right to restrict further processing or use of their personal data. Organizations have one month to respond to such requests.

e. **The right to data portability**- This right allows individuals to obtain a copy of their personal data, shared with the data controller, in a structured format and seek its portability to any other service provider or organization.

f. **The right to object** - Individuals have the right to stop their data from being used for any direct marketing. Organizations have one month to respond to objections received.

g. **Rights in relation to automated decision making and profiling** - Individuals have the right to challenge any automated decision making or profiling and where the same is not authorized or is without the individual's explicit consent.

What is data protection by design and by default under GDPR?

The GDPR aims to establish a culture of privacy by design and default. Data privacy should be considered in all the operational processes from the very start. Controllers should implement appropriate technical and organizational measures which are designed to implement the data protection principles and ensure that only personal data which is necessary for each specific purpose is processed.

What is Data Protection Impact Assessment (DPIA)?

Data Protection Impact Assessment (DPIA) is a process to help identify and minimize the data protection risks of a project. Organizations must undertake DPIA for any processing that is likely to result in high risk to individuals. This includes certain specified types of processing involving evaluation or scoring, automated decision making with significant effects, systematic monitoring, processing of large-scale data or sensitive data and use of any innovative technologies.

What are the provisions for appointment of Data Protection officer (DPO)?

GDPR requires organizations to appoint a Data protection officer (DPO), if their core activities require large scale, regular and systematic monitoring of individuals or involve a large scale processing of special categories of data or data relating to criminal convictions and offences.

The DPO shall be independent and report to the highest management level. The role of the DPO is to monitor internal compliance, inform and advise the organization on data protection obligations, offer advice regarding Data Protection Impact Assessments (DPIAs) and act as the key focal point for data subjects and the supervisory authority.

What are personal data breach notification requirements under GDPR?

A personal data breach means breach of security leading to the accidental or unlawful destruction, loss, alteration, unauthorized disclosure of, or access to personal data. Any such data breach is required to be notified by the data controller, within 72 hours of becoming aware of it. In 'high-risk' cases, the data controller needs to inform affected individuals. Data controller must keep a record of any data breach, including the facts, its effects and remedial action taken.

What are provisions relating to cross border data transfers?

GDPR imposes restrictions on transfers of personal data outside the European Economic Area (EEA), to ensure that the level of protection of individuals is not undermined. Transfers may be allowed, where Commission decides that a country meets adequacy requirements in terms of level of protection.

Transfers may also be permitted where the organization receiving personal data has provided appropriate safeguards. Appropriate safeguards include Binding Corporate Rules (BCRs) or model clauses approved by the Commission, compliance with approved codes of conduct and certification schemes.

5. India Privacy Regulations – IT ACT, RBI, TRAI

5.1 Information Technology Act

The primary objective of Information Technology Act (IT Act) enacted on 9th June'2000, was to facilitate E Commerce and provide a legal recognition to electronic documents and to provide a framework & mechanism for authentication through digital signatures. This was a sequel to passing of a model law on electronic commerce by the General Assembly of United Nations.

The amended act–Information Technology (Amendment) Act 2008, introduced penalties and compensations through clause-43 in Schedule IX, for any unauthorized access to computer systems and damage caused. It further introduced clause 43A for the protection of sensitive personal data, making any person or body incorporate liable for compensation up to INR 5 crores for any negligence in handling sensitive personal data and causing a wrongful loss or gain to any person.

'Where a body corporate, possessing, dealing or handling any sensitive personal data or information in a computer resource which it owns, controls or operates, is negligent in implementing and maintaining reasonable security practices and procedures and thereby causes wrongful loss or wrongful gain to any person, such body corporate shall be liable to pay damages by way of compensation, not exceeding INR five crore, to the person so affected'.

It further brought in penal provisions for dishonest & fraudulent acts pertaining to matters covered in section 43 and making such acts punishable with imprisonment up to three years or with fine up to INR five lacs or both.

Vide IT rules 2011, notified under Section 43A of the IT Act, Govt of India published 'Reasonable Securities Practices and Procedures' and 'Sensitive Personal data or information'.

The above rules define Sensitive personal data as information pertaining to;

- Password
- Financial information- Bank, Credit card, etc
- Physical, Physiological & Mental health
- Sexual orientation
- Medical records & history
- Biometric information

The IT rules place an obligation on anybody corporate or person handling & processing personal information or sensitive personal data to:

    a. **Publish privacy policy & disclose information**: Publish information pertaining to statement of practices & policies, type of personal & sensitive personal data collected, the purpose of collection & usage of such information and reasonable security practices & procedures followed.

b. **Collection of information**: Body corporate or person shall obtain consent from the individual regarding purpose & usage of such information. It shall use the information for the purpose it is collected and shall not retain the information for longer than is required for the purpose or otherwise required under any law. The provider of information shall have the right to have the information amended or withdrawn at any time. The body incorporate shall keep the data secure and shall have a grievance handling mechanism.

c. **Disclosure of information**: The body incorporate shall not transfer or disclose such data to a third party without prior permission, unless agreed under any contract or to meet any legal obligations or mandated under any law.

d. **Cross border transfer of data**: Cross transfer of data to any persons or entities abroad is allowed only if such country offers a similar level of data protection and the same is permitted under the contract or with the permission of information provider.

e. **Reasonable Security Practices and Procedures (RSPP):** The body incorporate or person shall implement RSPP that are commensurate to the criticality of information assets being protected and the nature of business. In the event of any breach, body incorporate shall be required demonstrate that it was complying such security control measures. Compliance to ISO 27001 standards and or any industry code best practices as approved by the Government are considered amongst reasonable practices.

5.2 RBI Guidelines on Customer confidentiality & Data protection

The Reserve Bank of India (RBI) is the Central Bank, which apart from its monetary functions carries on regulatory supervision over the Banking entities in India. Its objectives are to maintain public confidence in the system, protect depositors' interest and provide cost-effective banking services to the public.

RBI is mandated to promote and ensure safe, secure and efficient payment systems in the country and issue guidelines for best information security practices and technology risk management for Banks & financial institutions. Its key guidelines in brief, relating to customer data confidentiality & data protection are as under:

Customer Confidentiality

Banks, at the time of opening of accounts, collect KYC information of the customers. While complying with the above requirements, banks also collect a lot of additional personal information. The information provided by the customer for KYC compliance while opening an account is confidential and divulging any details thereof for cross selling or any other purpose is considered a breach of customer confidentiality obligations.

Banks are required to treat all customer related information as confidential. Any information about the customer for a purpose other than KYC requirements can be taken only on a voluntary basis and may be collected separately, after explaining the objectives to the customer and taking his or her express approval for the specific uses to which such information could be put.

The bankers' obligation to maintain secrecy arises out of the contractual relationship between the banker and customer, and no information should be divulged to third parties except for any disclosures under compulsion of law or required for public interest or where the disclosure is made with the express or implied consent of the customer.

Information Security, Electronic Banking, Technology Risk Management and Cyber Frauds (Gopalakrishnan Working Group Report)

Banks depend on the technology heavily not only for their smooth functioning but also for providing cutting-edge digital products to their consumers. Banks collect various personal data from customers for providing services. Banks, as owners of such data, should take appropriate steps in preserving the confidentiality, integrity and availability of the same, irrespective of whether the data is stored/in transit within themselves or with customers or with the third -party vendors; the confidentiality of such custodial information should not be compromised at any situation and to this end, suitable systems and processes across the data/information life cycle need to be put in place by banks.

RBI's report on Information Security, Electronic Banking, Technology Risk Management and Cyber Frauds, provides detailed guidance to Banks with an objective to strengthen IT governance & information Security.

Banks are required to have appropriate governance structure - IT strategy committees at board level and IT steering committees for oversight besides having defined & dedicated roles for managing information technology and risk viz. CIO, CISO etc.

Banks are required to have a separate cyber security policy, duly approved by their board, covering strategy to combat cyber threats given the level of complexity of business and acceptable levels of risk. All banks are mandated to set up a security operations centre (SOC) for continuous surveillance and keep regularly updated on the latest nature of emerging cyber threats.

Banks are required to report all cyber-security incidents to the Reserve Bank & CERT-IN (Computer Emergency Response Team– India, a Government entity). CERT-IN has also come out with national cyber crisis management plan and cyber security assessment framework. It covers four aspects: detection, response, recovery and containment.

Banks should take necessary preventive and corrective measures in addressing various types of cyber threats such as the denial of service, distributed denial of services (DDoS), ransom-ware, crypto ware, destructive malware, business email frauds including spam, email phishing, spear phishing, whaling, vishing frauds, drive-by downloads, browser gateway fraud, ghost administrator exploits, identity frauds, memory update frauds and password related frauds.

Storage of Payment System Data

There has been a tremendous growth in the digital payment ecosystem in the country. Entry of global players into India's digital payment space is expected to grow the segment by about five-fold to USD 1 trillion by 2023, as per the investment banking firm Credit Suisse report. Digital payments in India currently aggregate around USD 200 billion.

The major technology capabilities which have given a boost to digital payments include smart devices, Apps, near field communication protocol, QR code and mobile wallets. It enables the end consumer to conduct commerce with ease, flexibility and from anywhere.

The new payment systems are highly technology dependent and use innovative products and given the complexity & emerging threats need closer supervision. RBI has since Oct 15, 2018, mandated all system providers to ensure that the entire data relating to payment systems operated by them are stored in a system locally in India. This data should include the full end-to-end transaction details / information collected / carried / processed as part of the message / payment instruction. For the foreign leg of the transaction, if any, the data can also be stored in the foreign country, if required.

This is to ensure better monitoring and have unfettered supervisory access to data stored with these system providers as also with their service providers / intermediaries/ third-party vendors and other entities in the payment ecosystem.

5.3 Telecom Regulatory Authority of India (TRAI)

The Telecom Regulatory Authority of India (TRAI) is the regulatory body for the telecommunication sector in India. The key objective of TRAI is to provide a fair and transparent environment that promotes a level playing field and facilitates fair competition in the market.

India has a witnessed rapid expansion of telecommunications services and has been the focus area of Government of India's Digital India program to provide broadband connectivity across the villages and universal mobile access in the country. This has given a tremendous boost to connectivity and increased digital services in India.

Telecom and Internet service providers have access to a lot of information and data of their subscribers. This includes personal information including call detail records, calling patterns, location data, data usage information, etc. All telecom service providers in India are subject to various guidelines for the protection of user data. Apart from the provisions applicable under the Technology Act, 2000 (IT Act), there sector specific laws & guidelines for telecom sector.

The Indian Telegraph Act, 1885 (Telegraph Act) puts a general obligation on service providers to prevent unauthorized interception of messages and to maintain secrecy. There are restrictions on any kind of altering, intercepting or divulging the contents of any message, except as required by law. It is an offence to intercept a message with the intention of unlawfully learning the contents of any message, damage, tamper or prevent its transmission and fraudulently retain or detain a message. Further, the telecom service providers, under the unified license agreement, are required to take adequate safeguards to protect data of users. This includes protection of privacy of communication and to ensure that unauthorized interception of a message does not take place.

TRAI has also issued guidelines to put in place appropriate mechanisms to prevent the breach of confidentiality of information of subscribers and take steps for stopping unsolicited calls and bulk SMSs that pose a threat to consumer privacy by interfering with individual peace of mind and private life. A national customer preference register (NCPR) has been created to record preference of the subscribers and companies are prohibited from making unsolicited commercial communication with subscribers who have registered themselves in the NCPR.

6. Personal Data Protection Bill - An Overview

A committee of experts under the chairmanship of Justice BN Srikrishna was set up, with terms of reference to study various issues relating to data protection and to make specific suggestions on the principles to be considered for data protection in India and submit a draft data protection bill.

The Committee submitted 'Personal Data protection bill, 2018' to the Government of India, on 27th July'2018, for enactment.

The objectives of the bill are - creating a free and fair digital economy, respecting the informational privacy of individuals, and ensuring empowerment, progress and innovation.

The bill seeks to "protect autonomy of individuals in relation to their data, to specify where the flow and usage of personal data is appropriate, to create a relationship of trust between persons and entities processing their personal data, to specify the rights of individuals whose personal data are processed, to create a framework for implementing organizational and technical measures in processing personal data, to lay down norms for cross-border transfer of personal data, to ensure the accountability of entities processing personal data, to provide remedies for unauthorized and harmful processing, and to establish a Data Protection Authority for enforcement of provisions".

The main provisions of the Data Protection bill cover in details;

- Data Protection Obligations
- Grounds for processing of Personal Data
- Rights of the Data Principal
- Transparency & Accountability requirements
- Transfer of Personal data outside India
- Exemptions from provisions
- Data Protection Authority of India & Appellate provisions
- Penalties & Remedies and Offences

For a general understanding, various provisions of the bill are covered as FAQs below.

6.1 Where does the Data Protection bill apply to?

The Data Protection Bill applies to any entity or individual, undertaking processing of Personal data within the territory of India.

It shall also apply to data fiduciaries or data processors not present in India, but undertaking processing of personal data in connection with - any business carried on in India, or for any offering goods or services to data principals in India or in connection with any activity which involves profiling of data principals within the territory of India.

6.2 What are the Data Protection obligations in the Bill?

Data Protection obligations are the privacy principles that are a must for compliance by the Data Fiduciaries or processors in processing of personal data.

Various obligations stipulated in the bill are:

a) **Fair and reasonable processing** – The data should be processed in a fair and reasonable manner that respects the privacy of the data principal.

b) **Purpose limitation** - Personal data shall be processed only for purposes specified or for any other incidental purpose.

c) **Collection limitation** - The collection of personal data shall be limited to such data that is necessary for the purpose of processing.

d) **Lawful processing** - The processing of personal data is considered lawful only when it is based on consent of the individual. Processing of any sensitive data requires explicit consent of the individual.

   Other lawful purposes include - processing necessary for any functions of state that is authorized by law, or in compliance to any law or order of court, or for any prompt action in an emergency or for any employment reasons or any other specified reasonable grounds.

e) **Notice** - The data fiduciary shall provide the data principal with the following information, in a clear and concise manner, no later than at the time of collection of the personal data or, if the data is not collected from the data principal, as soon as is reasonably practicable, with regards to:

   - the purposes for which the personal data is to be processed,
     - source of data, if the same is not collected from the data principal,
     - period for which the personal data shall be retained,

- the individuals or entities with whom such data may be shared,

- Information on any cross-border transfer of such data,

- the identity and contact details of data fiduciary and data protection officer,

- rights of the data principal to withdraw such consent and procedure for the same,

- grievance redressal mechanism and

- any rating or data score assigned to data fiduciary (where applicable)

f) **Data quality** - The data fiduciary shall take reasonable steps to ensure that the personal data processed is complete, accurate, not misleading and is updated, having regard to the purposes for which it is processed. It shall inform to other individuals or entities to whom such personal data is disclosed or shared, of any such deficiency.

g) **Storage limitation** - The data fiduciary shall retain personal data only as long as may be reasonably necessary to satisfy the purpose for which it is processed. The personal data can be retained for a longer period, if such retention is explicitly mandated or to meet any obligation under a law.

h) **Accountability** - The data fiduciary shall be accountable for complying with the all obligations set out in the Data Protection act and should be able to demonstrate that any processing undertaken by it or on its behalf is in accordance with the provisions.

6.3 What are grounds for processing of personal data in Data protection bill?

The grounds for processing of personal data are the basic tenets of lawful processing.

Various valid grounds for processing of personal data are:

a. **On the basis of consent** - Personal data may be processed on the basis of the consent of the data principal, given no later than at the commencement of the processing. For valid consent, it must be;

- Free - meeting requirements & standards of Indian Contract act, 1872
- Informed – Provided with information as per the requirements of Notice provisions under the Data protection act (Section 8)
- Specific - with regard to the scope of consent in respect of the purposes of processing
- Clear - through an affirmative action
- Capable of being withdrawn

For the processing of any sensitive personal data such as passwords, financial information, sex, religion, an explicit consent is required. The data fiduciary must inform the data principal of any significant consequences as a result of such processing and provide a choice of separate consent to different categories of sensitive personal data relevant to the processing.

b. **For the functions of the State** - Personal data may be processed to meet:

- any function of parliament or any state Legislature
- any function of the state authorized by law, for provision of any services or state benefit or issuance any certification, license or permit.

c. **In compliance with law or any order of any court or tribunal** - Personal data may be processed if such processing is necessary to meet requirements explicitly mandated under any law or for compliance with any order or judgment of any Court or Tribunal in India.

d. **Processing of personal data necessary for prompt action** - Personal data may be processed if such processing is necessary to respond to - any medical emergency, epidemic or disaster involving a threat to the life or health of the data principal or other individual(s) or any breakdown of public order.

e. **For purposes related to employment** - Personal data of data principal, who is an employee, may be processed by a data fiduciary, as an employer, for the purpose of:

- recruitment or termination of employment of a data principal,
- provision of any service to, or benefit,
- verifying the attendance or
- assessment of the performance.

f. **For reasonable purposes** - Personal data may be processed for any other reasonable purposes, as may be specified. Such reasonable purposes would include:

- Prevention and detection of any unlawful activity including fraud
- Whistle blowing
- Mergers and acquisitions
- Network and information security
- Credit scoring
- Recovery of debt
- Processing of publicly available personal data

6.4 What are provisions relating to special personal & sensitive personal data of Children?

This category of data is sensitive and relates to vulnerable section and needs special protection.

The provisions stipulate that:

- Data fiduciary shall process personal data of children in a manner that protects and advances the rights and best interests of the child.
- Data fiduciary must have appropriate mechanisms for age verification and parental consent.
- Guardian data fiduciaries (who operate commercial websites or online services directed at children or who process large volumes of personal data of children) are barred from profiling, tracking, or behavioral monitoring or any targeted advertising directed at children.

6.5 What are the rights of data principals?

Various Data principal rights enshrined in the data protection regulations are:

a) **Right to confirmation and access -** The data principal shall have the right to obtain from the data fiduciary a brief summary of its personal data being processed, or that has been processed, and a brief summary of processing activities undertaken by the data fiduciary with respect to its personal data.

b) **Right to correction -** The data principal shall have the right to have its personal data corrected, updated or completed in case of deficient data. The data fiduciary shall also take reasonable steps to notify all relevant entities or individuals to whom such personal data may have been shared, regarding the changes in data.

Where the Data Fiduciary does not agree to undertake such correction, it will have to provide adequate justification, which can be disputed by the Data Principal.

c) **Right to Data Portability** - Where the data is processed through automated means, the data principal shall have the right to receive such data that has been provided to the data fiduciary or which has been generated by the data fiduciary in course of provision of goods or services or otherwise obtained or forms a part of any profile on data principal, in a structured, commonly used and machine-readable format.
It shall also have a right to have such data transferred to other data fiduciary in such a format.
This right is restricted and cannot be exercised, where the data processing is necessary for functions of the State or is in compliance of law or where compliance with the request would reveal a trade secret of any data fiduciary or would not be technically feasible.

d) **Right to Be Forgotten:** The data principal shall have the right to restrict or prevent continuing disclosure of personal data by a data fiduciary, related to the data principal, where such disclosure:
- has served the purpose for which it was made or is no longer necessary
- It was made on the basis of consent and such consent has since been withdrawn
- It was made contrary to the provisions of this Act or any other law

This will only be applicable, where the adjudicating officer determines that the rights and interests of the data principal override the right to freedom of speech and expression and the right to information of any citizen.

6.6 In what manner can the data principals exercise their rights?

To exercise any right, the data principal must submit a request in writing, to the data fiduciary, which shall acknowledge receipt of such request and comply within a specified time.

In case of refusal to comply with the request for any justified reason, the data fiduciary has to provide adequate reasons for such refusal and inform the data principal of its right to file a complaint. In the event of an unsatisfactory response or refusal, data principal can seek redressal of his grievance with data protection officer or approach Data Protection Authority.

6.7 What is 'Transparency & Accountability' under the Data Protection bill?

The transparency & accountability provisions lay down significant measures that a data fiduciary must adopt to demonstrate its compliance to the data privacy principles. This covers appropriate technical and organizational measures, as under:

a) **Privacy by Design** - Every data fiduciary must ensure that all personal data is processed transparently keeping the interest of data principal at every stage. All managerial, organizational, business practices and technical systems should be designed to meet the data protection obligations specified under the act and prevent any harm to the data principal.

The technology used in processing should be commercially accepted or should be of certified standards. There should be no compromise on privacy interests throughout the life cycle - right from the collection of personal data to its deletion.

b) **Transparency** - The data fiduciary shall maintain transparency in processing of personal data and make all information available as to:

- categories of personal data, manner of its collection and various purposes of processing such data,

- any significant risk to data during such processing,

- procedure for exercise of rights of data principal including a right to file complaints to the Data Protection Authority,

- any data trust score assigned to the data fiduciary, and

- any cross-border transfers of personal data

c) **Security Safeguards** - The data fiduciary shall implement appropriate security safeguards keeping in view the risks associated. It shall take steps - to protect integrity of personal data, prevent any unauthorized access and steps for encryption or de-identification of personal data. The security safeguards shall be reviewed periodically.

d) **Personal data breach notification** - The data fiduciary shall notify the Data Protection Authority of any personal data breach, in case such breach is likely to cause harm to any data principal. The notification shall cover nature of personal data and number of data principals impacted, possible consequences of the breach; and measures being taken by the data fiduciary to remedy the breach. The data fiduciary shall notify the Data Protection Authority, as soon as possible, within the prescribed time period.

The Data Protection Authority may ask the data fiduciary to take remedial steps and report the personal data breach to the data principal, after evaluating the severity of harm and any action required on part of the data principal to mitigate such harm.

e) **Data Protection Impact Assessment (DPIA)** - The data fiduciary shall undertake DPIA, before commencement of processing of personal data which involves - any new technologies or large-scale profiling or use of sensitive personal data or any other processing which carries a risk of significant harm to data principals.

The data protection impact assessment shall cover a detailed description of the proposed processing operation, the purpose of processing and the nature of personal data being processed. It shall include any potential harm that may be caused to the data principal and measures or remedial steps to be taken.

The data protection impact assessment report shall be submitted to the Data Protection Authority, who may after review direct the data fiduciary to cease such processing or impose conditions, in case the processing is likely to cause harm to the data principals.

f) **Record-Keeping -** The data fiduciary shall maintain accurate and up-to-date records of processing - important operations in the entire data life cycle, periodic review of security safeguards and data protection impact assessments, etc.

g) **Data Audits -** The data fiduciary shall get its policies and operations of personal data processing, audited annually by an independent data auditor.

The data auditor will evaluate the compliance of the data fiduciary with the provisions of Data protection act, covering:

- clarity and effectiveness of Notices,

- effectiveness of measures adopted relating to privacy of design,

- transparency in relation to processing activities,

- security safeguards adopted, and

- data breaches and response of the data fiduciary.

The Data Protection Authority shall register persons, with requisite qualifications, experience and background, as data auditors. It shall a specify procedure for conducting data audits and also prescribe penalties on data auditors for negligence.

A data auditor may assign a rating in the form of a 'Data trust score' to the data fiduciary, based on the audit and the criteria laid down for assigning a rating.

h) **Data Protection Officer -** The data fiduciary shall appoint a data protection officer with requisite qualification and experience. The role of data protection officer shall be:

- to advise the data fiduciary to meet its obligations under the Data protection act,

- undertake monitoring of personal data processing activities of the data fiduciary,

- advise on the data protection impact assessments and compliance with privacy design principles,

- assist & cooperate with the Data Protection Authority, on matters of compliance of the Data fiduciary, and

- be the point of contact for the data principal for any grievance handling.

i) **Processing by entities other than data fiduciaries -** The data fiduciary shall engage any data processor to process personal data on its behalf only through a valid contract. The data processor cannot further subcontract the relevant data processing to another entity without proper authorization, unless permitted in the contract.

The data processor shall treat all such personal data as confidential and process the data, as per the instructions of the data fiduciary or otherwise prescribed under any law.

j) **Grievance redressal** - Every data fiduciary shall have in place proper procedure and effective mechanism, to address grievances of data principals, efficiently and expeditiously.

A data principal may raise a grievance, in case of a violation of the provisions, which has caused or is likely to cause harm to such data principal, to the data protection officer or any other designated person, as applicable.

Data fiduciary shall resolve such grievances with in thirty days from the date of receipt. In case the grievance is not resolved or rejected or the data principal is not satisfied with the resolution, it shall have the right to file a complaint with the adjudication wing of Data Protection Authority. Further, any person aggrieved, by an order made by an adjudicating officer in this regard, may prefer an appeal to the appellate tribunal.

6.8 Who is a significant data fiduciary and what are its obligations?

The Data Protection Authority shall notify certain data fiduciaries or classes of data fiduciaries, as significant data fiduciaries, keeping in view the volume & sensitivity of personal data processed, turnover of the data fiduciary, potential risk of harm and use of new technologies in processing.

Such data fiduciary or class of data fiduciaries shall be mandatorily required to register with the Data Protection Authority.

All or any of the following obligations under the 'Transparency & Accountability provisions', as determined by the Data Protection Authority, shall apply only to significant data fiduciaries:

- Conduct of data protection impact assessments
- Maintenance of record-keeping
- Conduct of data audits
- Appointment of data protection officer

6.9 What are the provisions for cross-border transfer of data?

The cross-border transfer of any personal data for processing is allowed only on the basis of consent or explicit consent of data principal, as per the category of data.

Such transfer of data shall only be allowed to countries that meet adequacy norms- having adequate level of data protection in terms of laws and effective enforcement. The cross-border transfer may also be allowed on the basis of standard contractual clauses or Intra-group schemes, which shall be approved by the Data Protection Authority.

Where a transfer of personal data is undertaken on the basis of standard contractual clauses or intra-group schemes, the data fiduciary will certify and periodically report to the Data Protection Authority that the data transfer, made under the contract, adheres to such standard contractual clauses or intra-group schemes. It shall bear any liability for the harm caused, due to any non-compliance with the standard contractual clauses or intra-group schemes, by the transferee.

The transfer of sensitive personal data is allowed only in cases where such transfer is necessary for any prompt action relating to health or any other emergency services, subject to above conditions.

The data fiduciary is required to store at least one copy personal data on a server or data center located in India. Certain category of critical personal data, to be notified, shall be allowed to be processed only in a server or data center located in India.

6.10 What purposes are exempt from the provisions for processing of data?

There are select purposes which are exempt from various provisions of data protection bill. However, such processing will need to comply with provisions of 'fair and reasonable processing' under data protection obligations and 'security safeguards' expected under the transparency & accountability section.

Following purposes are exempt from various provisions:

a) **Security of the State -** Processing is allowed in the interests of security of state, with exemptions from various provisions. However, it should be as authorized under law and in accordance with the procedure established.

b) **Prevention, detection, investigation and prosecution under contraventions of law -** Processing is allowed to meet such interests, with exemptions from various provisions. However, it should be as authorized under law and in accordance with the procedure established.

c) **Processing for the purpose of legal proceedings -** Such processing is allowed where disclosure of data is necessary in such proceedings or for processing of personal data by any court or tribunal for judicial function. However, stipulations of provisions for 'cross border transfer of data' in addition to requirements of 'fair & reasonable processing' and 'security safeguards', will apply.

d) **Research, Archiving or Statistical purposes -** General exemptions apply for such purposes. However, stipulations of provisions for 'Data Protection Impact Assessments', in addition to requirements of 'fair & reasonable processing' and 'security safeguards', will apply. Further, such processing should not give rise to a risk of significant harm to the data principal or target the data principal specifically for any decision making.

e) **Personal or domestic purposes -** Such processing is exempt from all provisions, except the requirements of 'fair & reasonable processing'.

f) **Journalistic purposes -** General exemptions apply for such purposes. However, such processing of personal data should be in compliance with any code of ethics issued by Press Council of India or any media's self-regulatory body.

g) **Manual processing by 'Small entities' -** 'Small entity' is a data fiduciary with turnover up to 25 lacs and not disclosing or sharing data with any 3rd party and not processing personal data of more than one hundred data principals, in any one day in the preceding twelve calendar months.

Such entities are exempt from provisions relating to 'notice', 'data quality' and 'data storage limitations' under data protection obligations. Further, there are exemptions relating to 'right to data portability' & 'right to be forgotten' under data principals rights and provisions relating to 'transparency & accountability' of the data protection act.

6.11 What is the role of Data Protection Authority (DPA) of India and what are its powers?

The Central Government shall, by notification, establish 'Data Protection Authority of India'. The Authority shall be a body corporate and shall consist of a chairperson and six whole-time members.

The role of the DPA shall be to protect the interests of data principals, prevent any misuse of personal data, ensure compliance with the provisions of this Act, and promote awareness of data protection.

The key functions of the Data Protection Authority shall be:

- Monitoring and enforcing application of the provisions of this Act
- Taking prompt and appropriate action in response to a data security breach
- Categorization & registration of significant data fiduciaries & maintaining a database along with a rating in the form of a data trust score.
- Examination of any data audit reports submitted
- Registration of data auditors and maintaining a database of such registered data auditors and specifying the requisite qualifications, code of conduct, practical training and functions to be performed by such data auditors
- Monitoring cross-border transfer of personal data
- Issuing & approving codes of practice for promoting good practices of data protection and facilitate compliance with the obligations.
- Receiving and handling complaints

Various powers vested with Data Protection Authority - The Authority shall have the same powers as are vested in a civil court under the Code of Civil Procedure, 1908 and shall have following powers:

- **Power of Authority to issue directions** - It may issue directions to data fiduciaries or data processors, for its compliance.
- **Power of Authority to call for information** - It may require a data fiduciary or data processor to provide such information as may be reasonably required by it.
- **Power of Authority to conduct an inquiry** - The Authority may conduct an inquiry where the data fiduciary or data processor has violated any of the provisions of the act or where its activities are detrimental to the interests of data principals.
- **Search and Seizure** - In case of failure of any person to produce any books, registers, documents, records or data that have been called for or in case of likely tampering in any manner, the Data Protection Authority may exercise powers of search & seizure. It can authorize any officer of the designated level, to enter and search - premises, break open any lock, access any computer, computer resource, or any other device and seize all or any such books, registers, documents, records or data found, as a result of such a search.

6.12 What are various Penalties and Remedies specified in Data Protection bill?

Various levels of penalty have been prescribed, depending on the nature of violations:

a) The data fiduciary shall be liable to a penalty which may extend up to INR five crore or two percent of its total worldwide turnover of the preceding financial year, whichever is higher, in case of contravention of the following provisions by it, as applicable:

- Obligation to take prompt and appropriate action in response to a data security breach
- Obligation to undertake a data protection impact assessment
- Obligation to conduct a data audit
- Appointment of a data protection officer
- Failure to register with the Authority

b) There are more severe penalties for undernoted violations and data fiduciary shall be liable to a penalty which may extend up to INR fifteen crore or four percent of its total worldwide turnover of the preceding financial year, whichever is higher, in case of contravention of the following provisions by it, as applicable:
- Provisions relating to the data protection obligations
- Provisions of grounds for processing of personal data, sensitive personal data and personal data of children
- Failure to adhere to security safeguards as specified under 'Transparency & Accountability' provisions
- Transfer of personal data outside India in violation of conditions of cross border transfer of personal data

c) **Penalty for failure to comply with requests of Data principal under 'Data principal Rights'** - In case any data fiduciary, without any reasonable explanation, fails to comply with any request made by a data principal, it shall be liable to a penalty of INR five thousand for each day during which such default continues. This penalty is subject to a maximum of INR ten lac in case of significant data fiduciaries and INR five lac in other cases.

d) **Penalty for failure to furnish a report, return, information, etc.** - In case any data fiduciary fails to furnish any report required to be submitted, then it shall be liable to a penalty which shall be INR ten thousand for each day during which such default continues, subject to a maximum of INR twenty lac in case of significant data fiduciaries and INR five lacs in other cases.

e) **Penalty for failure to comply with direction or order issued by the DPA** - Failure to comply with directions or orders issued by DPA, shall invite a penalty which, in case of a data fiduciary may extend to INR twenty thousand for each day during which such default continues, subject to a maximum of INR two crore and in case of a data processor may extend to INR five thousand for each day during which such default continues, subject to a maximum of INR fifty lac.

f) **Penalty for contravention where no separate penalty has been provided -** In case of failure to comply with provisions as applicable to such person, for which no separate penalty has been provided, then such person shall be liable to a penalty subject to a maximum of INR one crore in case of significant data fiduciaries, and a maximum of INR twenty-five lakh in all other cases.

6.13 What offences are punishable under the Bill?

Following are cognizable offences and non-bailable under the provisions:

a) **Obtaining, transferring or selling of personal data contrary to the Act:** Any person who, in contravention of the provisions of this Act, obtains or discloses or transfers/sells personal data to another person, resulting in significant harm to a data principal, then such person shall be punishable with imprisonment for a term not exceeding three years or shall be liable to a fine which may extend up to INR two lac or both.

In case of sensitive personal data, such person shall be punishable with imprisonment for a term not exceeding five years or shall be liable to a fine which may extend up to INR three lac or both.

b) **Re-identification and processing of de-identified personal data:** Any person who, re-identifies personal data which has been de-identified by a data fiduciary or a data processor and or processes such personal data, without the consent of such data fiduciary or data processor, then such person shall be punishable with imprisonment for a term not exceeding three years or shall be liable to a fine which may extend up to INR two lakh or both. This shall not be applicable if the data belongs to the person charged with the offence or explicit consent has been taken from the concerned data principal.

6.14 What are the remedies available to the Data principals?

Any data principal, who has suffered harm as a result of any violation of any provision or rules prescribed, by a data fiduciary or a data processor, shall have the right to seek compensation from the data fiduciary or the data processor, as the case may be.

6.15 Who is an Adjudicating Officer?

The DPA shall have a separate adjudication wing for the imposition of any penalty or awarding compensation. The adjudication officer decides on the penalties & compensations, for any violation of provisions or offences under the act.

6.16 What is the adjudication process for deciding of penalties?

The adjudication officer shall impose a penalty as applicable, only after conduct of inquiry and giving reasonable opportunity of being heard. In determining the quantum of penalty, the adjudicating Officer shall have due regard to the following factors, as may be applicable:

- Nature, gravity and duration of violation
- Taking into account the nature, scope & purpose of processing concerned
- Number of data principals affected and the level of harm suffered by them
- Intentional or negligent character of the violation
- Nature of personal data impacted by the violation
- Repetitive nature of the default
- Transparency and accountability measures implemented
- Actions to mitigate the harm suffered by data principals
- Any other aggravating or mitigating circumstances such as, the amount of disproportionate gain or unfair advantage.

There is a right to appeal by an aggrieved party against an order by the adjudicating officer to the appellate tribunal.

6.17 What is the appellate process under the act?

There shall be an appellate tribunal, to hear and dispose of any appeal from an order of the adjudicating officer or any application against seizure of books, documents, records or data by the DPA.

The appellate tribunal may after providing the parties to the dispute or appeal, an opportunity of being heard, pass such orders thereon as it thinks fit. An order passed by the appellate tribunal under this Act shall be executable as a decree of a civil court.

An appeal against any order of the appellate tribunal shall lie to the Supreme Court of India.

6.18 What are major differences between 'Personal Data Protection Bill' & GDPR provisions?

The Personal data protection bill is broadly structured on the lines of GDPR, the major points of differences are as under:

a. **Terminology**:

The terms "Data Subject" & "Data Controller" as used in GDPR have been rechristened as "Data Principal" and "Data Fiduciary", to emphasize on the true nature of legal relationship between the two.

b. **Sensitive personal data:**

Personal Data Protection Bill considers password, financial data, transgender status, intersex status and caste or tribe, as sensitive personal data apart from other sensitive data elements mentioned in GDPR.

c. **Data principal rights:**

Right to be forgotten
- Under the Personal Data Protection Bill, the data principal has the right to restrict or prevent continuing disclosure of personal data by a data fiduciary subject to certain conditions. However, there is no provision to seek erasure of data.
- GDPR provides individuals the right to have its data erased subject to grounds for such erasure being fulfilled.

Right in relation to automated decision making
- There is no such explicit right in the Personal Data Protection Bill.
- GDPR provides individuals the right to challenge any automated decision making or profiling and where the same is not authorized or is without the individual's explicit consent.

Right to restrict processing
- There is no such explicit right in Personal Data Protection Bill.
- GDPR provides individuals the right to restrict further processing or use of their personal data, subject to certain conditions.

d. **Data breach notification:**

Under the Personal Data Protection Bill, the data breach notification to the individuals is required only when mandated by the DPA.

GDPR requires the data controller to notify the data subjects without undue delay in case where the breach is likely to result in a high risk to the individuals concerned.

e. **Data audits**:

Under the Personal Data Protection Bill, the data audits shall be done by independent auditors. The DPA shall register persons, with requisite qualifications, experience and background, as data auditors.

Under GDPR, the Supervisory Authority has the power to carry out any investigations or data audits.

f. **Cross border data transfers**:

The personal data can be transferred outside the territory of India only to countries that meet adequacy norms or under any standard contractual clauses or intra group schemes approved by the authority, subject to consent of the data principal.

GDPR additionally allows cross border transfer of data for the performance of a contract between the data subject and data controller. The consent of data subject is not a prerequisite, but is one of the basis for allowing such data transfer.

The data fiduciary is required to store at least one copy personal data on a server or data center located in India. Certain category of critical personal data, to be notified, shall be allowed to be processed only in a server or data center located in India.

GDPR does not impose any condition of storing copy of personal data locally.

7. Implementation & Compliance Approach

Data Protection Bill lays down the principles for processing personal data and provides specific rights to individuals with respect to their data. It further specifies remedies and penalties for unauthorized and harmful processing and lays down an enforcement framework. The data protection bill holds organizations accountable to process personal data in a fair and reasonable manner and take all steps to prevent any harm to individuals, as a result of such processing.

The data fiduciary needs to demonstrate that any processing undertaken by it or on its behalf is as per the provisions of this act. Failure to meet above obligations can make the organizations processing personal data, liable to a penalty which may extend up to INR fifteen crore or four percent of its total worldwide turnover of the preceding financial year, whichever is higher, as applicable.

The test of accountability lies both in implementing privacy guidelines and demonstrating compliance to specific obligations, as applicable to data fiduciary.

For implementation of data privacy guidelines, we suggest a 3-tier approach:

a) Develop a governance and privacy management framework

This entails the following steps:

- Define data privacy policy- with key objectives, covering all major areas of compliance such as data protection obligations, grounds for data processing, data principals' rights, transparency & accountability provisions and cross data transfers.

- Develop processes & procedures for compliance

- Define roles & responsibilities matrix

- Set up training, supervision & reporting mechanisms

b) Self-Assessment and Risk analysis

This shall involve determining the scope and applicability of data protection provisions, given the nature of data processing that the data fiduciary undertakes. It will further involve undertaking mapping and inventory of all personal data held by the organization, mapping data flows and undertaking a gap assessment.

Based on data mapping, an organization can undertake risk assessment and a categorise data as low, medium and high risk.

c) **Implementation & Compliance**

This shall include specific steps towards implementation of the data protection policies and showing compliance with provisions covering;

- Training & awareness
- Privacy notices
- Security safeguards
- Data protection officer
- Data impact risk assessments
- Data audits

The ensuing chapters elaborate the above approach and steps for implementation.

No one solution fits all. Organizations intending to take up privacy implementation should refer to detailed provisions, evaluate applicability and take professional help to meet compliance. The approach shared here is for a general understanding of the steps involved in implementation.

8. Privacy Management Framework

Governance lays down the accountability framework of any organization. It involves leadership support, organizational structure and processes to ensure that the organization complies with the regulatory guidelines and fulfills business strategies and objectives. It must address key risks faced by the organization. Effective governance is the responsibility of the Board of Directors and Executive Management.

Privacy is a key risk. Data breaches expose organizations to significant reputational and operational damage, as well as the possibility of legal action by the affected individuals. The data protection bill gives data principal the right to seek compensation, in case of any harm suffered by it, because of a violation of any provision under this Act.

Given the high risks of noncompliance, organizations will have to adopt a privacy compliance framework that can ensure data protection and provides regular reports and assurance to the management on the state of compliance across these organizations.

Personal data is a subset of the overall data or information held by any organization. Any framework to manage privacy risk must therefore be part of an overall framework for managing information risk.

ISO 27001 is an internationally recognized, management system standard for information security management. It describes the requirements of an Information Security Management System (ISMS) based on established best practices. It sets out controls and objectives to secure information and implement the requirements to meet their organizational objectives and risks assessed. And organization can also adopt ISO 27001 and get certification, which helps in providing assurance that it protects information assets.

As a part of the overall information security compliance, organizations must have a privacy management framework that covers all activities from collection of personal data, to its use, processing, retention and deletion. This will cover:

- Data protection policy- with key objectives covering all major areas of compliance viz. Data protection obligations, grounds for data processing, data principals' rights, transparency & accountability provisions, cross-border transfers, etc
- Process & procedures
- Roles & responsibilities matrix
- Training, supervision & reporting mechanism

8.1 Privacy Management Framework

Key Area/Objective	Action
Governance	
Review / revise policies and procedures	- Determine policies and procedures for in scope processing and assign policy owners
- Collate changes needed for each policy keeping in view data privacy provisions
- Approve and publish revised policies & procedures
- Conduct periodic review of ongoing changes
Organization structure	- Define roles & responsibility matrix for privacy implementation
- Form committees & review system
- Set up reporting mechanism
Training	- Design data privacy awareness & implementation programs, for staff
- Categorize different levels of employees
- Run an awareness campaign throughout the organization through mailers, extant guidelines, forum discussions and staff meetings, to create awareness and sensitize staff about privacy and their roles.

Data Protection and Privacy Implementation

Data Protection Obligations	
Data Collection & Use: • Process data in a fair & reasonable manner • Collect data for clear, specific & lawful purposes only • It complies with other principles – purpose limitation, Storage limitation & Data quality • The Privacy notice & information shared should be clear, concise and transparent.	• Establish what categories of information is collected • Identify personal data and sensitive personal data • Establish sources from which data is collected - online registrations, surveys, cookies (while browsing) • List down purposes for which data is used – validate its lawfulness • Any data used for marketing or profiling • Review of privacy notice to ensure the information shared is adequate and meets the notice provisions. • Review of the approach for how data is kept updated and accurate • Review how long the organization retains the data • Review process for deletion or anonymization of data
Grounds for Processing of Personal Data	
• Consent Process • The consent should be free, informed, specific, clear and capable of being withdrawn.	• Review consent forms • Review consent process - how consent is taken, withdrawn, documentation process, online consent options etc. • Evaluate whether the information shared is concise, clear and transparent and provided in an accessible manner • Establish effective audit trail- paper or online, to record how & when consent was taken • Set up mechanism for age verification & parental consent

Data Principal rights	
o The data principal can get a copy of the personal data held by the organization, have it suitably updated or corrected. o Individuals can seek personal details in a structured format and have the same transferred to any other data fiduciary or organization. o The data principal shall have the 'right to forgotten' and restrict or prevent any further processing of data or seek erasure of its data under certain conditions.	• Promote awareness about data principal rights through employee training and lay down reporting mechanisms to ensure compliance • Put in place systems & procedures to handle requests from individuals for access to their personal data and in the timeframe stipulated in the policy. • Define policy & procedure for data deletion, in line with the data retention policy or erasure of personal data at the request of individual • Lay down system for porting data to other organizations, on individuals request and sharing the same in a secure manner
Transparency & Accountability Measures	
Privacy by Design o Organization shall lay down managerial, organizational, business practices and implement technical systems so as to anticipate, identify, and avoid harm to the data principal.	• Review existing policies, systems & procedures, to ensure that data protection measures are a part of design and implementation of systems, services, products and there are built in safeguards to protect interests of data principals • Undertake complete data mapping and map data flows, to check vulnerabilities and risks at various stages of data processing and have access controls, data encryption and other Privacy Enhancing

o Organizations should protect privacy throughout data life cycle- from the point of collection to the deletion of personal data.	Technologies (PETS) implemented to mitigate risk • Ensure that any data processors engaged comply with the principles of data protection by design. • Evaluate technologies deployed to ensure that they meet the certified standards and are commercially accepted for nature of operations carried out.
Transparency o The organization will be transparent in its general practices related to the processing of personal data.	• Provide information related to processing in an easily accessible form through paper, online, website, etc. • Share all information related to nature of data collected, its purpose and use, any cross-border transfer and any data score assigned to the organization. • Identify any risk of harm to the data subjects in data processing and highlight the same in the information provided
Security Safeguards o The organization shall implement security safeguards that are proportionate to the risks associated with processing and likelihood and severity of the harm that may result from such processing.	• Identify and maintain a risk register and device safeguard mechanisms to protect confidentiality, integrity and availability of data through various measures such as: • Access Controls • Data Encryptions • High availability systems, IPS/IDS, etc. • Vulnerability assessments • Security Processes & Controls • Training users

Data Breach o The organization shall have well-defined system to notify the Data Protection Authority of any personal data breach related to any personal data processed by the data fiduciary where such breach is likely to cause harm to any data principal.	• Lay down procedures to detect personal data breaches and investigate effectively • Determine current practices in relation to data breaches and any gaps in reporting and notification procedures • Put in place mechanisms to notify affected individuals, where the breach is likely to harm to data principals
Data Protection Impact Assessment (DPIA) o The organization shall undertake DPIA prior to any processing involving new technologies or large-scale profiling or use of sensitive personal data, or any other processing which carries a risk of significant harm to data principals	• Document a DPIA process and train staff to create awareness and on how to carry out a DPIA • Describe the nature, scope, context and purposes of the data processing both within the organization and in any other processor organization engaged to process data and identify all associated risks • Identify measures that can eliminate or reduce high risks • Consult Data Protection Officer for advice and various other stakeholders in the DPIA process • Implement the measures that are outcomes of the DPIA and integrate the same in the project plan

Data Protection and Privacy Implementation

Record-Keeping ○ Maintain accurate and up-to-date records to meet legal requirements and show compliance with privacy provisions.	• Keep up-to-date record of various activities: ○ Categories of individuals and personal data collected and recipients of personal data ○ Records of consent ○ Privacy notices ○ Contract with third party processors ○ Any transfer of data to third countries including documenting the transfer mechanism & safeguards in place ○ Data retention schedules ○ Documented technical and organizational security controls to mitigate risks ○ Reports of Data Privacy Impact Assessments ○ Records of personal data breaches & notifications ○ Records of Data Audits, etc.
Data Audits • The organization shall have its policies and the conduct of its processing of personal data audited annually by an independent data auditor.	• Develop an audit plan in consultation with Data Protection Officer • The plan should cover all details related to - various categories of data collected, nature of processing, consent mechanism, privacy notices, privacy by design measures, security safeguards, etc • Undertake data audits internally by DPO or through an external auditor as required • Place audit report to the management committee • Track & remediate all deviations

	and observations
Data Protection Officer (DPO) o To appoint a data protection officer to carry out the various functions as defined.	• Designate a person with suitable qualifications & experience, as a Data Protection officer • Define role and responsibilities of data protection officer • Notify & publicize through Website, internal Circulars/mails and newsletters about the role & functions of DPO
Transfer of Personal Data outside India	
Cross Border Transfer of Data To comply with provisions related to cross border transfer of personal data	• Ensure to take data principal's consent for any cross-border transfer of data • Store locally a copy of data transferred • Notified critical data should be stored and processed only within the territory of India • Ensure that country or transferee organization meets adequacy norms • Have approved standard contractual clauses embedded in the cross-border transfer agreements and any intra-group schemes.

The privacy management framework should have an oversight mechanism for effective compliance. Most of the organizations have board level review committees for monitoring, apart from having a designated risk & privacy compliance executive. Having clearly defined metrics for reporting and evaluation process helps continuous improvement in compliance.

9. Data Mapping and Gap Analysis

9.1 Determining Scope & Obligations

Personal Data Protection Bill lays down various provisions & obligations, having regard to the category of data, specific purpose and nature of data processing. It prescribes additional obligations for the data fiduciaries that undertake high risk and high volume processing and there are exemptions for select purposes and type of entities as under:

- 'Significant Data Fiduciaries' - organizations engaged in processing sensitive personal data & having a high volume of processing activity or using new technologies, where the risk is high, must register with Data Protection Authority, appoint a data protection officer, maintain records of data processing, undertake data protection impact assessments and data audits.

- There are additional obligations of parental consent for processing personal data of children or handling other sensitive data.

- There are certain purposes such as — state security, research & statistical purpose, journalistic purpose etc. that are exempt from certain provisions.

- 'Small Entities' are exempt from provisions relating to notice, data quality, data storage limitations and various other data protection obligations.

So, the first step towards self-assessment & risk analysis is to determine the applicability of provisions and obligations that the organization has towards data processing undertaken by it.

Following questions will help in determining the applicability of provisions:

a. **Does the organization undertake processing of personal data within the territory of India?**

If yes, Personal Data Protection Bill provisions apply to such data fiduciaries.

b. **Does the organization process personal data in connection with - any business carried on in India, or for any offering goods or services to data principals in India or in connection with any activity which involves profiling of data principals within the territory of India?**

If yes, the Act applies to such data fiduciaries, even if the organization undertakes processing is located outside India.

c. **Does the organization fall under the definition of 'Guardian Data Fiduciary' - who operate commercial websites or online services directed at children or who process large volumes of personal data of children?**

If yes, organization must comply with additional obligations, as stipulated for such category of data fiduciaries.

d. **Does the organization fall under the definition 'Significant Data Fiduciaries' (based on volume & sensitivity of personal data processed, turnover of the data fiduciary, potential risk of harm and use of new technologies in processing)?**

If yes, there are additional obligations including registration with data protection authority that it must comply.

e. **Does the organization fall under the definition 'Small Entity' - with turnover up to 25 lacs and not disclosing or sharing data with any 3rd party and not processing personal data of over one hundred data principals, in any one day in the preceding twelve calendar months?**

If yes, there are certain exemptions from certain provisions for small entities.

f. What is the purpose of processing personal data and is the purpose exempt from certain provisions?

If yes, there are certain exemptions from certain provisions for specified purposes.

9.2 Data Mapping

Data mapping is an essential exercise to document all personal data that an organization collects and processes. It would not be possible to undertake a privacy risk assessment, unless an inventory of all personal data maintained by the organization is made and mapping done to document data flows within and outside the organization.

Data discovery can be done in various ways. There are many tools available for data scanning that can help map data location, volume, encryption, and broad classification. The other common method used for data discovery is through questionnaires and interactions with various owners managing applications and business processes. Further, a study of the current list of assets (applications, databases & file systems), data protection policies, business process documents, data sharing & processing agreements, shall help prepare data inventory and understand data flows.

The approach to data discovery can either be application centric or business function wise. The priority can be decided based on the basis of volume & sensitivity of data handled. The nature of questions & stakeholders will depend on type of business function or process that is sought to be covered.

An indicative list of questions that can help capture relevant data can be:

- What personal data organization collects?
- What is the source and manner of data collection?
- Are the individuals given privacy notice or information?
- What is the purpose of data collection & how is the data processed?
- What steps must the organization take to ensure accuracy of data or keep it updated?
- Who all can access data and is there any sharing of data internally and with external entities?
- What modes organization uses for data transfer or sharing?
- How and where is data stored?
- How long does the organization keep data and when and how is it deleted?
- How is the data at rest and data in transit safeguarded?
- Is there any cross-border transfer of data?
- How does the organization meet an individual's data access & other requests?
- Is the personal data used to run any advertising & marketing campaigns?

The ultimate aim of data collection is to build a data inventory and map process linkages with the data elements that help in understanding various category of data, applicability of data privacy principles, status of compliance and risks. A data inventory can be in a tabular or Excel-based representation.

Various data elements and the attributes that can be collected are illustrated as under:

• Details of Data Fiduciary	Name & Contact details
• Data Protection Officer or Representative	Name & Contact details
• Application or Business Function	Name of Application or Business Unit
	Application/Business owners
• Business Process	Name of business process
	Process owner
• Personal Data	
Individual ID Information	Name
	Address
	Place of Birth
	Date of Birth
	Gender
	Nationality
	Passport Number
	National Identity Number

	PAN / Tax Id Number
	Employee Id
	Tel / Mobile Number
Family data	Marital status - Married/Single
	Parents Details
	Number of Children
• Education, Employment & Professional Activity Data	School
	College / University
	Name of Employer
	Salary etc.
• Financial Data	Name of Bank
	Account Details
	Card Details, etc.
• Health Data	Medical History
	Insurance Details
• Biometric Data	Finger Print
	Retina Scan
• Category of Data	Personal Data
	Sensitive Personal Data
	Children Data
	Critical Data
• Category of individuals	Employees, Customers, Suppliers, Vendors

• Consent	Yes or No
• Privacy notice	Yes or No[
• Data Retention Period	Number of Years
• Location of data	Name of Location
• Data Stored locally or not	Yes or No
• Data Encryption 　　　Storage 　　　Transit	Yes or No Yes or No
• Access Control	Yes or No
• Cross-Border Data Transfer	Names of Country BCR Intra Group Scheme

9.3　Gap analysis

A compliance checklist and its implementation status shall help in making an assessment of risk & identify areas where the organization has a gap in compliance.

A granular checklist may have all the applicable provisions of the data protection, listed along with requirements and a compliance check for assessment. A high-level assessment may be done against major obligations that require compliance by the data fiduciary.

An illustrative list of questions for the checklist is as under:

a. Does the organization have a documented data protection & Information security policy?
b. Does the organization conduct data protection awareness training for all staff?
c. Does the organization document data inventory to record what data does it hold and where?
d. Does the organization record the lawful basis of processing personal data?
e. Does the organization have a proper system to record consent for processing personal data?
f. Does the organization have a system to identify age and record parental consent for personal data of children?
g. Does the organization have a privacy notice for the data it is processing and is privacy information shared concise, simple & accessible?
h. Does the organization have a system to record various requests of data principals regarding their personal data (for access, rectification, erasure, portability etc) and respond to them with in time lines specified?
i. Does the organization have a proper grievance handling mechanism?
j. Does the organization have a system to identify the requirement and undertake data privacy risk assessments?
k. Does the organization incorporate privacy by design principles in its managerial, organizational, business practices and technical systems?
l. Does the organization have in place appropriate security safeguards- data pseudonymizations, encryptions, access controls and other data loss prevention measures to protect data?
m. Does the organization have a system in place to detect and notify any personal data breaches to the authority?
n. Does the organization get its policies and operations of personal data processing, audited annually by an independent data auditor?
o. Does the organization maintain accurate and up-to-date records of processing?

p. Does the organization have data sharing agreements with processors & third parties, with clauses for the safeguarding of personal data?

q. Does the organization ensure adequacy level of protection and have approved BCR or Intra company group contracts for any cross-border transfer of data?

9.4 Risk Assessment

The data mapping exercise and gap assessment will help measure risk and compliance. The risk is the product of the likelihood of an undesirable event and the severity of the impact of that event. The safeguards that an organization must comply should be proportionate to the risk. The organization needs to identify the threats and vulnerabilities that form a risk, determine the likelihood and impact of the risk materializing and apply controls to mitigate these risks.

Personal Data Protection Bill identifies a certain category of data and its processing as 'high risk' and imposes stricter obligations on the data fiduciaries. Data protection regulations define risk to personal data from the perspective of harm to individuals and categorizes following as high risk:

a. Processing of sensitive data

b. Processing involving a high volume of personal data

c. Using automated means for decision making or profiling

d. Processing involving new technologies

The risks under the data protection provisions could emanate from violation of various data protection provisions relating to handling of personal and sensitive personal data. From an overall information security perspective, the risk needs to be evaluated from the point of view of confidentiality, availability and integrity of data.

The nature of risks will vary based on the category of data, purpose & scale of data processing, examples of risks could be:

Confidentiality	Availability	Integrity
Unauthorized data access	Loss or destruction of data	Technology - hardware & software
Physical security breach	Systems - hardware, applications, Netowork available or down	Data corrupted
Staff unaware of security controls	Media destroyed or lost	Un-authorized data changes
Weak encryptions	Systems compromised- virus attack, denial of service attacks etc	Faulty systems or programs
Lack of access controls	Back up failure	Poor version control

The risk identification process can be done through:

- Analogy - Review risk assessments from other similar projects
- Historical - Examine lessons learned documents or knowledge database
- Interview – Conduct interviews with subject experts
- Interview stakeholders – Application & business owners, subcontractors, suppliers etc.
- Project / process documents - Analyze data mapping & flows

To assess the level of risk, one needs to consider both the likelihood and severity of harm. Structured matrix of likelihood and severity of harm, would provide an objective assessment of overall risk levels as - Low (low probability-low impact), Medium (High probability-low impact) & High (High probability- High impact).

The above assessment will help quantify risk exposure and decide on various risk mitigation measures required in terms of improved governance, training and security safeguards to be implemented.

10. Key Steps – Privacy Implementation

10.1 TRAINING

Employee training is one of the most important elements of compliance for data protection. The employees should understand the sensitiveness of data privacy as well as the financial and reputational risks that the organization is exposed to in the event of any data breach. Employees need to know their role in data protection and its criticality to the business.

An important component of the Personal Data Protection bill is 'privacy by design', requiring organizations to adopt managerial, organizational, business practices and technical systems that anticipate, identify and avoid harm to the data principal. This includes processes and procedures that employees must comply. Training and staff awareness go a long way in creating a compliance culture within the organization.

The data fiduciary must demonstrate, as a part of accountability provisions, that it complies with all obligations and any processing undertaken by it or on its behalf is in accordance with the provisions of this Act and all safeguards have been taken to ensure data privacy protection. The data fiduciary is required to maintain accurate and up-to-date records pertaining important operations relating to data processing and periodic review of security safeguards, to demonstrate compliance. Staff training and keeping an appropriate record of various trainings is an important element of demonstrating compliance to the provisions.

Training should cover all staff at various levels:

- Board & Top Management
- Managers
- Line Staff
- Technical Staff

The training curriculum shall depend on the staff level & and nature of functions performed. The training could be to create awareness, core implementation, refresher training, etc.

An indicative training curriculum, given below, shall help organizations plan for data privacy training.

Training Curriculum

Level	Domain / Area	Contents
Board & Top Management Managers Line Staff Technical Staff	Personal Data Protection Act - An Over View	• Data Privacy & Terminology • Privacy Principles & Data Protection Obligations • Consent & Data Principal Rights • Penalties & Fines • Data Breaches • Data Protection Impact Assessments • Data Protection Officer • Cross Border Data Transfers

Audience	Topic	Content
Board & Top Management Managers	Governance	- Major Risks and IT Framework - Governance Framework for Data Protection - Data Protection Policy - Roles & Responsibilities - Training & Awareness Building - Data Protection Officer - DPIAs - Data Principal rights - Data Audits
Board & Top Management Managers	Compliance framework	- Evolving Compliance Requirements - Security Safeguards
Managers Line staff Technical staff	Data Privacy Bill Provisions	- Data privacy & Global Framework - Privacy Principles & Data Protection Obligations - Grounds for Processing of Personal Data - Sensitive Personal data & Data of Children - Rights of Data Principals - Accountability & Transparency provisions - Cross Border Data Transfers - Penalties & Compensations

Managers Line staff Technical staff	Data Privacy Implementation	• Roles & Responsibilities • Data Protection Policy • Data Collection & Use • Consent & Use • Data Retention, Erasure, Anonymization • Data Principal Rights • Privacy by Design • Transparency- Privacy Notices • Security Safeguards – Access Controls, Encryptions, Data Protections & Availability • Conduct of Data Audit • Data breach handling • DPIA • Records Maintenance • Cross Border Data Transfer -Adequacy, CBR & Intra Group Schemes
Managers Technical staff	Technical Controls	• Identity & Access Managements • Data Encryptions • Other Privacy Enhancing Measures • ISO 27001, Industry Codes & Practices, Sector Specific Controls PSS-DSS / TRAI / RBI

10.2 PRIVACY NOTIFICATION

Personal Data Protection Bill lays accountability on data fiduciaries for complying with the obligations laid down in the bill and to demonstrate that any processing undertaken by them or on their behalf is in accordance with the provisions of this Act.

'Notice' (Section 8) and 'Transparency' (Section 30) are some of the overreaching obligations that the data fiduciary must comply. It is about providing individuals with clear and concise information about what data fiduciary does with their personal data and what kind of information must be shared and the manner it should be provided to the data subjects.

A privacy notice is an important document that an organization must publish to provide information about processing of personal data and rights of data principals.

Information to be shared with the data principals:

a. **The data fiduciary shall provide the data principal with the following information:**

- Name & contact details of the data fiduciary and the contact details of the data protection officer, if applicable;
- The categories of personal data being collected;
- The source of such collection, if the personal data is not collected from the data principal;
- The purposes of the processing
- The lawful basis for the processing
- Any risk of significant harm during processing of data
- The individuals or entities with whom such personal data may be shared

- Details of any cross-border transfer of the personal data that the data fiduciary intends to carry out
- The retention periods for personal data
- The rights of data principal and the manner in which they may be exercised
- The right to withdraw such consent (if applicable)
- The procedure for a grievance redressal
- The right to file complaints to the Authority;
- Any rating in the form of a data trust score that may be assigned to the data fiduciary

b. **Time when privacy information should be shared**

- Data fiduciary shall provide individuals with privacy information at the time they collect their personal data from them.
- In case the personal data is not collected from the data principal, then the information should be shared with the concerned individual, within a reasonable period.

c. **Manner in which the privacy information should be provided**

- The data fiduciary shall provide the information under the provisions to the data principal in a clear and concise manner that is easily comprehensible to a reasonable person.
- Options should be provided to view the document in the common languages of the regions where the service is available.
- The acceptance to the terms or permissions should be on Opt-in basis requiring an affirmative action to be taken by the user instead of opt out and with no pre-checked boxes.

10.3 Data Protection Officer (DPO)

Personal Data Protection Bill stipulates appointment of DPO by the data fiduciaries. This requirement is part of the 'Transparency and Accountability' measures and is mandatory for a category of organizations designated as 'significant data fiduciaries' which process large volume of personal or sensitive personal data and undertake processing involving risk of harm to data principals or use of new technologies.

Organizations can also decide to have a DPO as a good practice or for greater assurance.

In case of data fiduciaries not present within the territory of India and carrying on processing to which the act applies, such organizations must appoint DPO who shall be based in India.

This requirement to appoint data protection officer has also been stipulated under GDPR and various other data protection acts.

DPO is a focal person for data protection in an organization and point of contact for the data principals for grievance redressal and to the Data Protection Authority for compliance related matters. The contact details of the DPO should be published and also communicated to the Data Protection Authority.

The DPO can be a dedicated person or have a shared responsibility depending on the size of the organization. There should be no conflict of interest in its responsibilities. This can also be outsourced to an external 3rd party service provider having requisite expertise.

The DPOs should have a sufficient degree of autonomy and be in a position to perform their duty in an independent manner. GDPR grants a degree of protection to such officers against dismissal or penalizing for performance of their tasks.

Role of Data Protection Officer

The role of the data protection officer shall be:

a. Providing information and advice to the data fiduciary on matters relating to fulfilling its obligations under the Act;

b. Monitor personal data processing activities of the data fiduciary to ensure that such processing does not violate the Act;

c. Advise the data fiduciary, where required, on the manner in which data protection impact assessments must be carried out, carry out the review of such assessment and submit the assessment report to the DPA.

d. Provide advice to the data fiduciary, where required on the manner in which internal mechanisms may be developed in order to satisfy the principles set out for privacy by design.

e. Shall be a point of contact with the Authority DPA on matters of compliance of the data fiduciary within the provisions under this Act;

f. Shall be a point of contact for the data principal for the purpose of raising grievances to the data fiduciary

g. Maintain an inventory of all records maintained by the data fiduciary as required under provisions for record keeping as per the transparency & accountability provisions.

Eligibility and qualification requirements

The data protection officer shall meet eligibility and qualification requirements, as specified. The general guidance for the position of data protection officer is as under:

- The data protection officer should have professional qualities and have a good knowledge of the data protection & privacy laws.

- DPO should preferably have knowledge of industry or sector and processing activities

- The data protection officer must be independent and report to the highest level of management.

- It should not have a conflict of interest or role in its position. However, it may be assigned other functions without compromising its core responsibilities.

- The data protection officer should be well supported with resources and given appropriate access to processing activities for due performance of its role.

General Job Descriptions for Data Protection Officer:

The general job description for the role of DPO, as published by various organizations, for such positions, is as under:

Qualification & experience:

- A legal, compliance, IT security or audit background
- In-depth knowledge of data protection and privacy laws and familiarity with privacy and data protection risk assessment best practices and methodologies

- Requisite educational qualifications & industry experience
- Should have any data privacy professional certification: Certified Information Privacy Professional (CIPP), Certified Information Privacy Manager (CIPM), Certified Information Systems Security Professional (CISSP), Certified Information Security Manager (CISM) and Certified Information Systems Auditor (CISA)
- Integrity & high professional ethics and maintains a high level of confidentiality and trust
- Good communication skills & stake holder management
- Change management & project management experience
- Good understanding of data processing activities and information systems and security
- Experience in data protection, Information governance and managing IT systems

Jobs & responsibilities:

- Drive implementation of essential elements of the data privacy regulations
- Responsible for advising on the measures to be taken to meet compliance under privacy regulations
- Shall be a point of contact for regulatory authorities and data principals (subjects)
- Maintain data protection policies and procedures and oversee the maintenance of records required to demonstrate data protection compliance
- Supervise and advise data protection impact assessments
- Manage a program of awareness-raising and training to foster data privacy culture and compliance
- Assist in the data incident response and data breach notification procedures.

- Assist in risk assessments to identify potential threats that could cause unauthorized disclosure, misuse, alteration or other compromises and propose remediation steps.
- To monitor, track and keep a record of all data processing activities, risk assessments, privacy by design activity and the exercise of data principal (subject) rights
- To audit compliance with regulatory requirements & privacy laws and engage other stakeholders to ensure effective deployment of policy, practice, business and technology
- Periodic reporting to management on compliance reports & reviews
- Disseminate best practice guidance and updates from Data protection authorities and various forums across, within the organization
- Engage with staff and stakeholders at various levels for creating awareness and understanding of the regulations, data subject rights and the data fiduciary (controller) obligations.

10.4 Data Protection Impact Assessment (DPIA)

Data fiduciaries are required to undertake DPIA before commencement of any processing of personal data which involves - new technologies or large-scale profiling or use of sensitive personal data or any other processing which carries a risk of significant harm to data principals.

DPIA is a tool to help identify and minimize the data protection risks of new projects and processes involving new technologies. Similar provisions for conduct of DPIAs exist in GDPR and other data protection acts.

Criteria for DPIA

The DPIA must be done in all such processing, which is likely to result in high & significant risk to the data principals. European Data Protection Board (EDPB) has suggested the following nine criteria for assessing such risk:

a. **Evaluation or Scoring** - This includes profiling and predicting an individual's behavior, preferences, interests, performance, financial or economic condition. This may also involve tracking geo-location & movements of individuals.

b. **Automated-Decision making** – This kind of processing leads to decision making about individuals without application of human discretion or judgment. This may lead to exclusion or discrimination against individuals and result in denial of service, opportunity or benefit.

c. **Systematic Monitoring** - Any process used to observe, monitor or control data subjects (principals) and any systematic monitoring of a publicly accessible area. In such processing, personal data may be collected without the knowledge of individuals and who have no control on such data being collected and may not be aware how the same will be used.

d. **Sensitive Data -** This would include an individual's political opinions, medical records, geo-location data, financial data, biometric & genetic data.

e. **Data processed on a large scale -** Processing of a large volume of data considering the number of individuals, the variety of data, duration and geographical extant.

f. **Matching or combining datasets** - Processing involving combining, comparing, or matching personal data obtained from multiple sources and collected for different purposes.

g. **Data concerning vulnerable data subjects** – Processing involving data of children, employees or other vulnerable segments of population viz. elderly, patients, asylum seekers. This is considered a high risk on account of imbalance of power or their ability to give clear consent with understanding.

h. **New technologies** - processing involving the use of new technologies like Internet of things or innovative use of existing technologies including AI. The use of new technology can involve new ways of data collection and usage with potential high risk to individuals.
i. **Data subject rights** - Processes that impact the data subject rights to access a service or entry into a contract.

DPIA Coverage & Steps

A data protection impact assessment should broadly cover:

a. Details of the processing operation, purpose of processing and the nature of personal data being processed,
b. Identify and assess risk of harm to individuals, and
c. Identify measures to mitigate the risks.

Various steps involved in DPIA process shall be:

a) **Identification of the need for a DPIA**: This should cover the key objectives of the project identified for DPIA and type of processing it involves. The need and justification for undertaking DPIA should be recorded having regard to various criteria for such processes.
b) **Description of processing** - It should describe the entire life cycle of the data processing, right from the stage of data collection to its processing and deletion. The personal data from all sources and applications needs to be mapped, data flow across the organization needs to be created, processes and users to be defined and any interfaces with other applications within or outside the organization must be documented. It should highlight who all have access to the data, if any data is shared, any new technologies or innovative methods used in the processing or security measures adopted and if the processing identified as likely high risk in the project.
   - **Scope of the processing** - It should highlight the nature and type of the data. It should also highlight any sensitive personal data used in the processing, volume and scale of data processed, geographical coverage and the time of data retention.

- **Context of the processing**: It should cover nature of relationship with the individuals and the control they have on data and expected use of their data. It should capture details, of any data of children or other vulnerable groups, used in processing and any concerns over this type of processing, the technology used or security.
- **Describe the purposes of the processing**: This should describe the objective of data processing, the intended effect on individuals and the benefits of the processing sought to be achieved.

c) **Consultation Process**: Data Protection Officer is the key stake holder to be consulted. Other stakeholders include various asset and process owners, security persons, other business experts.

d) **Compliance to data protection provisions**: This should cover nature of compliance followed to ensure the lawful basis for processing, purpose limitation, and steps taken to ensure data quality and data minimization. It should describe the rights available to individuals and how they can enforce them including grievance mechanism. It should further include any measures taken for compliance of obligations by the processors and safeguards for any international transfers.

e) **Risk Identification:**

The risk assessment should consider both- the security risks to confidentiality, integrity & availability of personal data and potential impact of data processing on the individuals by way of:

- Inability to exercise rights and to access services or opportunities
- Discrimination or any other significant economic or social disadvantage
- Loss of control over the use of personal data
- Identity theft or fraud
- Financial loss
- Reputational damage
- Physical harm
- Loss of confidentiality
- Re-identification of pseudonymized data

Apart from above, corporate risk in terms of compliance, brand or reputational damage and financial risk needs to be evaluated.

To assess the level of risk, one needs to consider both the likelihood and severity of the possible harm. Structured matrix of likelihood and severity of harm, would provide an objective assessment of overall risk levels as - Low, medium & high risk.

f) **Risk Mitigation**

Various risk mitigations could be considered so as to reduce or eliminate risks identified:

- Improve governance for data security- have clear role & responsibilities and documented processes & procedures
- Training of staff to increase awareness
- Additional technological security measures such as - encryptions, access controls, data loss prevention
- Restrict collecting certain types of data

- Reducing the scope of the processing
- Reducing retention periods
- Anonymizing or pseudonymizing data
- Using a different technology
- Data sharing agreements with suitable clauses for data privacy protection
- Transparent & comprehensive privacy notices
- Improved process & controls for breach detection & notifications

The additional costs likely to be incurred along with benefits of each measure will help provide a cost benefit analysis and enable decision making.

g) DPIA Outcome

The outcome of the assessment exercise would be to record

- All additional measures required to mitigate or address each risk
- Level of residual risk after above measures and its acceptance
- Consultation with Data protection officer for go ahead on the processing and any difference in opinion should also be recorded
- In case of high risk persisting- consultation with the Data protection authority before go ahead with processing

10.5 DATA AUDIT

Annual data audit is one of the key requirements under the Accountability & Transparency provisions of the Personal Data Protection Bill.

Data audit is mandatory for the data fiduciaries classified as 'significant data fiduciaries' based on turn over criteria, the volume of personal data or sensitive personal data handled, any risk of harm in processing and use of new technologies in processing. Such data fiduciaries shall have its policies and the conduct of its processing of personal data audited annually by an independent data auditor under this Act.

Following are the key parameters and indicative check points that may help the organizations to plan for a data audit or self-assessment.

a. **Clarity and effectiveness of privacy notices**

- Weather the notice contents are in clear language, concise & easily comprehensible to a reasonable person
- Transparency – clarity about data collected, purpose, data subject rights, grievance redressal, data sharing, data retention, any risk of harm in processing, any cross-border transfer of data, any rating in the form of a data trust score and contact details of data fiduciary & data protection officer
- Easy navigability & multilingual support
- Updation of privacy policy
- Permissions & acceptance to terms

b. **Effectiveness of measures under Privacy by design**

- Managerial, organizational & business practices - policies and procedures, organizational structure, roles and responsibilities, training and awareness

- Technical systems - physical security, operations security, communications security, asset management, access control, incident management, business continuity, audits and vulnerability testing reports
- Fulfillment of the data protection provisions - fair and reasonable processing, purpose limitation, collection limitation, lawful processing, notice, data storage limitation & accountability
- Technology used is commercially accepted or meets certified standards

c. **Security safeguards adopted**

- Data confidentiality - data anonymization and encryption methods deployed
- Data integrity - application & physical access controls, process control eg maker checker, etc.
- Data availability - physical security, operations security, communications security, business continuity
- Periodic review of its security safeguards by the data fiduciary

d. **Data breaches & promptness of notification**

- Maintaining a record of data breaches
- Prompt notification of the data breach to the DPA along with details of incident - nature of data breached, the number of data principals affected and possible consequences of breach
- Remedial actions to mitigate the impact & a prevent recurrence of such incidents

10.6 SECUIRTY SAFEGUARDS

Security safeguards are very important for protecting confidentiality, integrity and availability of information. Poor information security can expose systems and data to risk and vulnerabilities, which can result in loss or unauthorized processing of personal data and cause harm to individuals. Examples of harm to individuals could be:

- Identity thefts
- Loss, destruction, unauthorized access and modification of personal data
- Targeting & profiling of individuals
- Damage to individual reputation
- Loss of opportunity or denial of service
- Financial loss

Data privacy bill lays down specific obligation on organizations to implement appropriate security safeguards having regard to the nature, scope and purpose of processing of personal data, the risks associated with such processing, and the likelihood and severity of the harm that may result from such processing. The security safeguards shall include:

- use of methods such as de-identification and encryption
- steps necessary to protect the integrity of personal data; and
- steps necessary to prevent misuse, unauthorized access to, modification, disclosure or destruction of personal data.

The nature of appropriate or reasonable security measures has not been defined in the data protection bill. However, the SPD Rules which have been issued under Section 43A of the IT Act, that deal with data security, define reasonable security practices.

As per the Rule 8–(Reasonable Security practices & procedures) defines "reasonable security practices as the implementation of security practices and standards, a comprehensively documented information security program, and information security policies that contain managerial, technical, operational and physical security control measures commensurate with the information assets being protected and the nature of the business".

While there is no prescription on nature of security guards to be implemented under the data protection provisions and other such regulations, implementation of best practices based on ISO 27001 standards and codes of best practices recommended by recognized industry institutions, as applicable, is considered a good step towards demonstrating compliance to the provisions.

ISO 27701 (Security techniques – extension to ISO/IEC 27001 and ISO/IEC 27002 for privacy information management – Requirements and guidelines) has been published recently in Aug'2019. It aims to fill assurance gap and provides an integrated approach to privacy information management system (PIMS) as a part of information security management system (ISMS), by prescribing additional controls that relate specifically to data protection and privacy

ISO/IEC 27001:2013

ISO/IEC 27001 is an information security standard, published by the International Organization for Standardization (ISO) and the International Electrotechnical Commission (IEC), jointly.

ISO/IEC 27001:2013, which is the latest version of the standards, specifies the requirements for establishing, implementing, maintaining and continually improving an information security management system (ISMS). It also includes criteria for assessment and treatment of information security risks.

ISO/IEC 27001 provides a holistic approach to managing information security– protecting confidentiality, integrity and availability of information and data. The ISMS framework has 114 controls in 14 clauses and 35 control categories. Organizations can adopt the above standards or use them as guidance for implementing information security management systems. The scope of the ISMS shall depend on the specific area of operations or organization, which has been identified for implementation, based on the risk assessment. The relevant security safeguards or controls for the specific area and risks shall be adopted.

The readers should refer to ISO/IEC 27001:2013 standards for detailed guidance and any implementation. For a general understanding, shared below is a summary of broad domains covered under the standards:

a. **Information Security Policy**
- The organization should have a documented information security policy document duly approved by management. The policy should be published and communicated to all employees and relevant external parties
- The information security policy shall be reviewed at planned intervals or when significant changes occur, to ensure its continuing suitability, adequacy, and effectiveness.
- Appropriate process for contacting authorities (regulators, law enforcement agencies etc), should be laid down, specifying responsible persons and circumstances under which they must contact these authorities.

b. **Organization of Information Security**

- All information security responsibilities shall be defined and allocated. Conflicting duties and areas of responsibility shall be segregated to reduce opportunities for unauthorized or unintentional modification or misuse of the organization's assets.

- The use of mobile devices- smart phones, laptops, tablets, as BYOD (bring your own device) at workplaces is increasing vulnerabilities associated with these devices. A policy and supporting security measures shall be adopted to manage the risks introduced by using mobile devices. The security measures required to be implemented include - regular data backups for stored sensitive data, physical security measures, secure communication methods for transmitting data such as Virtual Private Network, updates for operating system and other software, access control, data encryption and deployment of anti-virus systems.

- Teleworking (employees working away from the office, i.e., outside of the physical premises of the organization) exposes the organization to risk of unauthorized access of sensitive information by a third person remotely or loss/theft of devices. Information can be intercepted during transmission between the organization and the device. Also an outdated device can be compromised and used to invade the organization's systems. Through this policy, an organization can establish the rules as to who may telework, which services or information can be accessed by teleworkers, what access controls to be established - password, two-factor authentication, use of VPN how devices shall be configured, protected, and used.

c. **Human Resource Security**

- Proper screening and background checks need to be carried out prior to employment. This would include background checks for contractors as well.
- The job agreements with employees and contractors shall include organization policies and their responsibilities for information security.
- All employees and contractors should comply with the IS policies and procedures of the organization. They should be given awareness education and training, as relevant for their job function
- There shall be a formal and communicated disciplinary process in place to take action against employees who have committed an information security breach.
- The responsibilities and duties of employees or contractor, that remain valid after termination of employment, shall be defined and communicated to them and enforced.

d. **Asset Management**

- An inventory of all the information assets shall be maintained and ownership assigned for each asset.
- There should be restricted access to assets through 'acceptable usage policies. This should incorporate approval process for access, an authentication procedure, access control List and labeling of devices,
- All employees and external party users shall return all the organizational assets in their possession upon termination of their employment, contract or agreement.

- Information shall be classified in terms of legal requirements, value, criticality and sensitivity to unauthorized disclosure or modification. For example, information could be classified as public, confidential or secret, to determine the authorized access and disclosure allowed or assets could be classified in terms of criticality to business operations as - low, medium or high.

- An appropriate set of procedures for information labeling and handling of assets shall be developed and implemented in accordance with the information classification scheme adopted by the organization.

- Procedures shall be implemented for the management of removable media in accordance with the classification scheme adopted by the organization. Media shall be disposed of securely when no longer required, using formal procedures. Media containing information shall be protected against unauthorized access, misuse or corruption during transportation.

e. **Logical Security / Access Control**

- An access control policy shall be established, documented and reviewed based on business and information security requirements. User's access to resources- Information, computers & devices, applications, network etc., should be on 'need to know or use' basis. Principle of least privilege based on the role rather than unlimited access, should be implemented.

- The access controls should be implemented through a formal registration process and provisioning of access rights for all user types to all systems and services. A formal user registration and de-registration process shall be implemented.

- The allocation and use of privileged access rights shall be restricted and controlled. Asset owners shall review users' access rights at regular intervals

- The access rights of all employees and external party users to information and information processing facilities shall be removed upon termination of their employment, contract or agreement.

- Users shall be required to follow the organization's practices in the use of secret authentication information.

- Access to information and application system functions shall be restricted in accordance with the access control policy. Where required by the access control policy, access to systems and applications shall be controlled by a secure log-on procedure.

- Password management systems shall ensure quality passwords with a minimum number & type of characters required as per the password policy. It should enforce password expiry and failed log-in attempts controls. The use of utility programs that might be capable of overriding the system and application controls shall be restricted and tightly controlled. Access to program source code shall be restricted.

f. **Cryptography**

- A policy on the use of encryption and cryptographic controls for protection of information shall be developed and implemented.

- The policy should identify business requirements for which encryption must be used, having regard to criticality of data and risk associated. Encryption can have an impact on the resource utilization and slow down the processing & transmission of information, if adequate provisioning of resources is not done. So, the counter effects of encryption and benefits must be evaluated while deciding on the encryption policy and nature & level of encryption to be used. Legal or sector specific guidelines for encryptions must be complied.

- The encryption & decryption involves use of mathematical keys. Controls in creation, distribution, changes, backups and storage of the cryptographic key material, is very critical to plug any vulnerability in this area.

g. **Physical and environmental Security**

- Security perimeters (barriers such as walls, card-controlled entry gates or manned reception desks) shall be used to protect areas that contain information and information processing facilities such as data centers and other places hosting sensitive information. Secure areas shall be protected by appropriate entry controls to ensure that only authorized personnel are allowed access.

- Physical protection risks against damage from fire, flood, earthquake, explosion, civil unrest, and other forms of natural or man-made disaster shall be evaluated and protective measures implemented.

- Physical protection and guidelines for working in secure areas shall be designed and applied. Access points such as delivery and loading areas and other points where unauthorized persons may enter the premises shall be controlled and, if possible, isolated from information processing facilities to avoid unauthorized access.

- Equipment should be installed and sited as per the OEM recommendations and protected to reduce the risks from environmental threats and hazards as well as opportunities for unauthorized access.

- To ensure continued availability of equipment and protect its integrity, it shall be properly maintained and protected from power outages and other disruptions caused by failures in supporting utilities. Redundancy in power supply, DG & UPS backups, dual or multiple source of network connections and routing, should be implemented, for high availability of systems.

- There should be safe disposal of all electronic media. All items of equipment containing storage media shall be checked to ensure that any sensitive data and licensed software has been removed or securely overwritten prior to disposal. Users shall ensure that unattended equipment has appropriate protection. A clear desk policy for papers and removable storage media and a clear screen policy for information processing facilities shall be adopted.

h. Operations Security

- Operating procedures shall be documented, maintained, and made available to all the users concerned. Documented procedures help in a consistent and effective operation of systems.

- Changes to information processing facilities and systems shall be controlled and should be subject to change management process.

- The use of resources viz. data storage capacity, Processing & computational power and communication capacity (bandwidth), must be monitored for effective capacity management and proactive provisioning, so that operations are not impacted.

- Development, test and operational environments shall be segregated to reduce the risks of unauthorized access or changes to the operational system.

- Detection, prevention, and recovery controls to protect against malicious code must be implemented. Timely patching of software to reduce vulnerabilities and up-dation of the malware protection systems is a must for better protection. There should be user awareness around the usage of removable media and use of unauthorized software.

- Back-up copies of information and software shall be taken and tested regularly in accordance with the agreed backup policy.

- Audit logs recording user activities, exceptions, and information security events should be enabled and logs maintained for an agreed period. Event logs help in incident management, auditing and access control monitoring.

- Logging facilities and log information shall be protected against tampering and unauthorized access. System administrator and system operator activities shall be logged. The clocks of all relevant information processing systems within an organization or security domain shall be synchronized with an agreed accurate time source.
- There shall be procedures in place to control the installation of software on operational systems and appropriate hardening done to avoid vulnerabilities.
- Periodic and timely vulnerability assessment must be done and appropriate measures taken to address the associated risk.
- Audit requirements and activities involving checks on operational systems shall be carefully planned and agreed to minimize the risk of disruptions to business processes.

i. **Communications Security**

- Networks shall be adequately managed and controlled in order to protect systems and applications using the network and maintain security of information flowing through the network. Various technical controls include connection control, end point security, firewalls, Intrusion detection/prevention systems, access controls list and other physical & logical controls.
- Segregation of the network should be done for a group of users or services to improve control & security.

- Additional controls in the form of encryption controls, cryptographic controls, must be placed to secure information in transit. Transfers of business Information, between the organization and any 3rd party should be through formal agreements incorporating transfer policies & procedure and technical controls should be deployed in line with the risk associated, for its secure transfer.

- The network service agreements with service providers must have an appropriate level of service levels (SLAs) and security levels defined to meet the business requirements.

j. **System acquisition, development and maintenance**

- Any new requirement of information systems, or enhancements to existing information systems, should take in to consideration need for security controls.

- The information flows over public networks should be protected from fraudulent activities, unauthorized disclosure and modification. Sensitive data and financial transactions data should be protected through secure protocols, encryptions & implementation of other security safeguards.

- Software development should follow secure coding practices and security needs should be taken in to consideration at all stages of software development. This shall involve hardening of software applications, version controls and use of secure repositories. Outsourced software development shall be supervised and monitored by the organization.

- All changes to the software environment should follow strict change management process. This includes evaluation, approval process, implementation & review. The changes must be thoroughly tested, to ensure that there is no adverse impact on operations & security and the same should be implemented only after due acceptance. Record of testing done should be maintained for audit purpose.

k. **Supplier relationships**

- Organizations should undertake segmentation of suppliers based on value and risk and apply supplier management controls accordingly.
- Agreements with third party service providers should cover all relevant security requirements. Any changes in information policies must be brought to knowledge of Suppliers.
- The services, reports and records provided by the third party should be regularly monitored and reviewed, and audits should be carried out regularly.
- Changes to supplier services should consider supplier type & relationship, criticality of business systems and processes involved and re-assessment of risks.

l. **Information Security Incident Management**

- Develop and implement processes for preventing, detecting, analyzing and responding to information security incidents.
- Employees, contractors and other 3rd party service providers should be made aware of their obligations to report security incidents. They must note and report any observed or suspected security weaknesses in systems.
- All information security incidents must be documented and reported immediately to the designated information security administrator & appropriate authorities (e.g., regulator, law enforcement agencies etc).
- All Information security events must be must be logged and classified based on severity.
- Assign owners for timely resolution and root cause analysis.
- Once an incident has been resolved, necessary changes must be made in the system, including any change in policies & procedures required. Further, knowledge data base should be updated for future learning and reference.
- In case of a security incident warranting legal or disciplinary action, due care must be taken in the collection of evidence and its preservation, as per the defined rules.

m. **Business Continuity**

- Disruptions and failures of IT facilities can impact business. Events that can cause interruptions to business processes shall be identified, along with the probability and impact of such interruptions and their consequences for information security.

- Business continuity plans shall be tested and updated regularly to ensure that they are up to date and effective.
- Adequate redundancy must be provided in Information processing facilities, to meet the high availability requirements

n. **Compliance**

- All relevant statutory, regulatory and contractual requirements should be explicitly defined, documented and kept up to date.
- There should be a periodic review of the organization's policies, processes, and procedures for information security or when significant changes occur in the environment.
- Managers must ensure compliance to all security procedures, security policies and standards and the same should be checked periodically for conformity.
- Important records should be protected & retained, in accordance with statutory, regulatory, contractual, and business requirements.
- Compliance to Data protection and privacy regulations must be ensured.
- Cryptographic controls shall be used in compliance with all relevant agreements, laws, and regulations.

10.7 Privacy Enhancing Technologies

Privacy enhancing technologies (PETs) broadly refers to the use of technology to help achieve compliance with data protection legislation. It includes both applications to be used by individuals to protect themselves and applications that can be used by organizations to support privacy and data protection for individuals. These are technologies that can help minimize the collection and use of personal data and facilitate compliance with data protection rules. The use of PETs should result in making breaches of certain data protection rules more difficult and/or helping to detect them.

The PETs include technologies & techniques generally applied to achieve confidentiality, integrity & availability (CIA) of data and specific measures required to achieve principles of data privacy- data limitation/minimization, Identification, authentication & authorization, pseudonymization & anonymization of data, encryptions. These techniques can be applied after due assessment of risk and evaluation of tools that may be suitable for a level of risk and costs & other factors involved.

Few key technologies and techniques used include:

a. Identity & Access management

Identity & access management (IAM) primarily helps in authentication of a person or a device and in limiting its access to the data or resources.

The identity management system involves a person sharing his credentials and password to authenticate. The authentication is a process of validating a person's identity through an identity management service, before permitting access to the resources.

The type of authentications to establish the identity of a person, is based on:

- Some things you know- User id, Password, Secret question, etc

- Something you have–Device, token, access card or USB, etc

- Something you are-Biometrics- finger print, retina scan

Single or multiple level authentications can be prescribed depending on the level of protection needed. So, one may have User id & password and an additional requirement of OTP sent on a device that is registered with the service provider/application or requirement of biometric authentication apart from having access card etc, to gain access.

After identification occurs, the authorization has to take place to ensure that the user has legitimate access to a resource or perform an action. This is sought to be done through access control.

Access Control list (ACL) is a list of identities associated with a resource that indicates types of permissions allowed to a resource. The access is granted on the basis of the principle of least privileges that are required to execute a function. This limits the access to 'need to know basis' and the individual cannot access data or resources that he is not required to for the nature of job that he is required to perform. This also limits the damage if the credentials of the person are compromised or hacked. This access control could be on user based or group-based rules. This is sought to be achieved through either Discretionary Access Control (DAC)- in which every resource is mapped to a list of users who can access it or Mandatory access control- where the access is mapped to set of levels and users are linked to specific access level.

There are single sign-on systems (SSO) that allow authentication across applications or services, which makes users convenient as they are not required to keep separate user id & password for each application.

b. Encryptions

Data encryption is an important technique in protection of personal data and safeguarding confidentiality of information. Encryption is a method by which plain text data (unencrypted) is converted by using an encryption key (a mathematical function) in to a encoded unreadable format called the cipher text. The cipher text can be read only when decrypted with a correct key.

Encryption prevents unauthorized access to data and unlawful processing, as only the person who has the encryption key can decrypt & access the data. The encryption can be used as a protection to both for data storage- data at rest or for data transfer- data in transit.

Types of encryption - Symmetric and Asymmetric

In Symmetric encryption the same key is used for encryption and decryption. Key has to be shared with the recipient of data to enable it to decrypt and read. It is therefore critical that a secure method is considered for transferring the key between sender and recipient. The most widely used symmetric key is AES (Advanced Encryption standard).

Asymmetric encryption, also known as Public key cryptography uses a key pair -a different key is used for the encryption and decryption process. One of the keys is typically known as the private key and the other is known as the public key. Public Key is shared with the public and the private key is kept secret by the owner. Data encrypted with the recipient's public key can only be decrypted with the corresponding private key. This takes away the risk of compromising the encryption key while sharing and data transfer can be done without the risk of unauthorized or unlawful access.

Levels of encryption

Encryption can be at Field level, Record level, File level or Disk level, depending on the nature of data sought to protected and level of protection needed. A more granular level of encryption offers greater security as the extent of data that can get compromised gets minimized.

In field level encryption, sensitive fields such as the credit card number, account number or social security number, where a part of the number can be encrypted to protect the sensitive data.

In File encryption, sensitive files can be encrypted or one can place a group of files within an encrypted container.

A full disk encryption shall encrypt the entire contents of the disk and is useful against risk of device being stolen or lost. Most of the operating systems offer this functionality and the same needs to be configured using the setting options.

Personal data under the transfer from one device to another across internet or wired or wireless connection is exposed to risk of interception and encryption provides protection. Encryption is particularly recommended while transmitting over wi-fi & unsecured public networks. Implementation of VPN (virtual private network) or TLS (transport layer security) at network level provides the necessary protection during the transmission. This will encrypt only the data in transit, for a safe storage at the recipient end, it will need separate encryption.

There are sector specific guidelines for complying with the minimum standard for encrypting personal data eg PCI-DSS (Payment card industry data security standard) specifies use of strong cryptography and security protocols such as SSL/TLS, SSH or IPSec, to safeguard sensitive cardholder data during transmission over open, public networks.

Safeguards to be adopted in encryption

The data can be decrypted using the symmetric keys and private keys, it is critical that the encryption keys are kept secure & secret. There is a need for an effective key management system. The keys should be periodically replaced & fresh keys generated to re-encrypt the data, to avoid any compromising of the key.

Data has to be decrypted before it can be read or processed and so there are chances of its being accessed in an unauthorized manner during the processing. Other access controls & safety measures, including staff training & awareness are required to ensure its safe keep during processing.

Any malware attack on a device or if an application having access to data, gets compromised, it shall expose the data to risk even if it is encrypted, it's important to have due malware protection and undertake periodic vulnerability assessment of the applications to mitigate any risks identified.

c. Pseudonymization & Anonymization of data

Pseudonymization refers to the process of de-associating an individual's identity from its personal data being processed, by replacing one or more personal identifiers, i.e. pieces of information that can allow identification (such as e.g. name, email address, mobile number, social security number), relating to an individual with the so-called pseudonyms, such as a randomly generated values.

Pseudonymization can support data protection in different ways. It can hide the identity of the individuals, so that it is not easy to connect the data with specific persons. It also increases the level of difficulty for a third party to correlate the breached data with certain individuals without the use of additional information. The distinction between anonymized and pseudonymized data is that pseudonymous data can be re-identified, while anonymous data cannot be re-identified.

Pseudonymization does not remove the identifying information from the data but merely reduces the link ability of a dataset with the original identity of an individual through encryption, masking or any other technique. While in anonymization, the identifying information is removed, so that the remaining personal data cannot be linked to the individual. From regulatory compliance perspective, the anonymized data is not categorized as personal data and is hence exempt from its provisions. Pseudonymized data thought not exempt, but offers a degree of protection and is considered as one of the safeguards in data protection measures.

Various Techniques used for Pseudonymization & Anonymization of data are as under:

- Encryption: Encryption of an individual's identifiers - such as e.g. name, email address, mobile number, social security number, can be an effective method to generate pseudonyms. The original identifier of a data subject can be encrypted to create a cipher text that is to be used as a pseudonym.

- Tokenization: refers to the process that the data subjects' identifiers are replaced by randomly generated values, known as tokens, without having any mathematical relationship with the original identifiers. Hence, knowledge of a token has no usefulness for a third party, i.e. any other than the data fiduciary or processor.

- Masking: refers to the process of hiding part of an individual's identifier with random characters or other data. For example, a masked credit card, bank or social security number may be transformed in the following way: 7648 5421 2800 8933 >> XXXX XXXX XXXX 8933.

- Scrambling: refers to general techniques for mixing or obfuscating the characters. The process can be reversible, according to the chosen technique. For example, a simple permutation of characters may be such a scrambling, e.g. a credit card or social security number may be transformed as follows: 7648 5421 2800 8933 >> 3018 3024 9846 8257.

- Blurring: refers to use an approximation of data values, to reduce the precision of the data, reducing the possibility of identification of individuals. The value could be rounded to the nearest multiple.

d. Anti-tracking tools or browser extensions

The risk of one being tracked while browsing is very common. It is a serious breach of privacy as there is lot personal information being collected without consent. Tracking is done by advertisers of products that one may have visited earlier. Other means viz. cookies -a piece of data inserted into your browser, or a MAC address or location data can be used to track an individual and what the person is doing on web.

Apart from various privacy settings on browsers, there are a number of anti-tracking tools or add-ons, that blocks cookies and stop advertisers and other third-party trackers from secretly tracking where you go and what pages you look at on the web. If an advertiser seems to be tracking the user on multiple websites, the loading of content from that source is blocked. Various tools allow users to check what trackers are following them and decide which ones to allow and which ones to block.

e. Digital Rights management

Digital Rights Management (DRM) applications are programmed to protect electronic copyright for digital media. DRM allows the content owner to encrypt media, data, e-book, content, software, or any other copyright material. Only those with the decryption keys can access the material. There are tools that can limit or restrict what information users can access and what rights they have. DRM allows the owner of the content to:

- Restrict or prevent users from editing, printing, sharing or forwarding the content
- Restrict use or access after the specified date
- Restrict access to certain IP addresses, locations or devices
- Maintain an audit trail of persons & times the content was downloaded or accessed.

Given the above functionality, the DRM besides protecting copy rights, can be used to control access to confidential information and sensitive personal data and there by assist in data privacy management.

11. INDUSTRY PERSPECTIVE ON DATA PRIVACY & PROTECTION

In this section, we bring to you the industry perspective on data privacy and new data protection bill and the specific challenges that various industry leaders foresee in its implementation.

We have collated this feedback through a structured questionnaire, from CEOs and industry leaders of various sectors- consulting organizations, banking, mutual Fund, NBFCs, health and education. Few of the sectors-Banking, Health and BPO, having global business operations, have already been exposed to privacy regulations with implementing of GDPR and hence are ahead in the learning curve. These sectors are also under regulatory supervision from various regulators such as RBI, SEBI, TRAI and hence subject to various controls including relating to data protection, confidentiality and Information security.

The questionnaire sought feedback on Data protection bill, challenges foreseen in implementation of its provisions and in particular for MSME/SME sector, likely costs involved, current data protection measures deployed by the organizations, business process changes and additional measures in terms of technology & tools that are required to meet compliance of new provisions.

General Views about the Data Protection Bill

The respondents have welcomed the draft bill and believe that this is a step in the right direction and shall augment the data privacy laws in India. This will have a positive impact on the industry, as it will help create trust with various stakeholders. The new regulations will make the industry compliant to global standards on data privacy and provide assurance to global clients on safeguarding of its data processed by Indian firms and our global delivery centers. The requirements on purpose limitation, collection limitation and privacy by design, are considered big positives and the organizations will have to revisit the entire data life cycle–collection, processing and use, storage, transmission, archival and disposal, to comply with the new requirements.

However, there are concerns that disproportionate compliance requirements may negatively impact the Indian start-up and SME ecosystem. There are apprehensions regarding various provisions relating to data localization, grounds for processing, data breach & notification requirements, criminal liability and the definition of "sensitive personal data".

It is felt that mandating data localization would undermine the competitiveness of Indian start-ups, SMEs, e-commerce firms, FinTech and other technology driven firms. They would not be able to leverage global cloud technologies and cutting-edge analytics solutions that require free flow of data platforms. This could potentially harm India's multibillion IT outsourcing business.

The grounds for processing of personal data should also include contractual necessity-processing necessary for the performance of a contract. The requirement to obtain an additional consent for cross border transfer should be considered unnecessary as that would put additional administrative burden.

The data breach notification requirement to the DPA should only be in case of significant risk of material harm to the data principals.

It is felt that provisions relating to storage limitation which would involve data deletion are hard to comply. These should be revisited and there may be restrictions on use rather than insisting on deletion.

The provisions relating to criminal offences are considered draconian. There should be overall cap on penalties and criminal offense provisions should be revisited as the imprisonment of individuals for any violations is considered excessive.

Sensitive personal data definition should be restricted to special risks in relation to discrimination of individuals and abuse of fundamental rights. Passwords, official identifiers & financial data do not fall under this special category and should not be categorized as sensitive personal data.

Sector specific impact

The bill is considered sector agnostic, however, sectors such as the IT-BPM, telecom, health, hospitality and BFSI, which have exposure to global privacy regulations like GDPR, are better placed to deal with the compliance requirements, as the provisions of the bill are similar. Many of these sectors are also under regulatory supervision from various regulators and hence are at more mature state from the point of view of governance & compliance.

Challenges foreseen & Cost involved in implementation

On specific challenges foreseen with compliance of new provisions, it is felt that the data protection bill will increase the cost of compliance. The requirements for notice, consent and grounds of processing personal data and sensitive personal data, will force the organization to redesign their core systems, get fresh consent, and change the data practices that will eventually increase the cost of compliance. Provisions such as privacy-by-design, data protection impact assessments, storage limitations, data localization and stringent security measures will carry additional onus.

Multiple versions of the data stored in multiple systems across the organization and data mapping exercise of each customer is considered challenging.

The implementation of data protection provisions may call for changes in business processes & require putting in place additional technical controls towards identification of sensitive personal data, prevention and proactive detection of information security incidents & data breaches. It shall also require a review of existing contracts with third parties and targeted training of employees & contract workers, to inculcate a culture of respecting privacy of personal data and compliance to provisions.

The cost involved in implementation would vary based on the organization and the provisions that the entity is subject to. Complying with changing regulatory provisions, requires incurring substantial costs, exposure to potential regulatory action or litigation, and may require changes to business practices. These costs may be disproportionate for the MSME/SME sector and pose a greater challenge for small businesses, as they lack organization structure, tools & processes for such compliances.

Current data protection provisions & practices

The industry today is subject to various provisions of the IT Act, 2000 and the SPD Rules (Sensitive Personal Data and Information, 2011) for ensuring data protection. Besides, various regulators such as RBI, TRAI, IRDAI & SEBI have also stipulated guidelines for various entities towards safeguarding the confidentiality & integrity of personal data.

In line with regulatory guidelines, the organizations are reported to have comprehensive documented information security program and information security policies that contain managerial, technical, operational and physical security control measures. Many organizations have adopted controls as per the ISO27001, to ensure that customer's personal information is protected against any unauthorized access, processing or erasure. Banks are also additionally complying with the PCI-DSS in protecting the card data.

The IT framework implemented in these organization includes, application controls, user management & access controls, business rules controls, interface controls, data center environment controls, LAN authentication, desktop hardening controls, operating system and database controls, etc. Organizations carry out periodic trainings of staff on information & cyber security practices.

Key focus areas for data privacy compliance

Foremost part for compliance is governance. Many organizations form exclusive steering committees during the implementation phase to closely monitor the progress and have the ongoing reviews done by the risk & compliance committees.

Organizations need to have visibility over the personal data they have collected. Once this inventory and classification is achieved, an impact assessment of the privacy risks would go a long way in setting up the security framework to comply.

Data deletion strategy must be adopted keeping in view the business needs for data retention and any statutory requirements. A clean desk policy and proper storage of all the documents is must to avoid any data breach. In case of data processing by 3rd party or any sub processing, there should be proper documentation incorporating all obligations for personal data protection. All existing outsourcing contracts must be reviewed and supplementary contracts should cover requirements as per the data protection regulations.

Organizations also need to focus on building dedicated data privacy teams to deal with the execution of data subject rights and creating processes to handle breach notification requirements.

The privacy by design principle would require changes to the IT architecture, to ensure that privacy principles are embedded at all stages - application development, technology deployment and implementation.

The data management systems being the repository of key business information will need adequate cyber security measures and redundancy backups to ensure data security and integrity.

In summary, the respondents have overall welcomed the provisions and have shared their concerns on challenges expected in compliance.

The individual feedback from the respondents is covered in the following section.

11.1 Som Mittal, Former President and Chairman, NASSCOM

1) **How do you look upon the data protection bill proposed for the Indian Industry or organizations?**

    The Bill and the Srikrishna Committee Report ("**Report**") provides a much-needed framework for data protection and privacy in the country. Building upon the work of Justice A.P. Shah Committee, and the re-statement of the fundamental right to privacy by the Supreme Court of India in K.S. Puttaswamy v. Union of India, the Bill is a step towards creating a sector-agnostic data protection framework, which calls for all stakeholders to be more responsible and build trust in dealing with personal data. The requirements on purpose limitations, collection limitations, and importance given to new age regulatory principles such as privacy by design are big positives but present compliance challenges that need to be recognised and addressed. Specifically, disproportionate compliance requirements are likely to negatively impact the Indian start-up and SME ecosystem. Further, in the context of India as a global IT hub, the proposed law needs to provide greater comfort to global clients in terms of processing of their data by Indian firms as well as data processing by the Global Capability Centres (GCC).

2) **What specific challenges do you foresee for its compliance in the Indian context given the experience of GDPR implementations at many organizations.**

    We foresee challenges with respect to the implementation of data subject rights and achieving privacy principle level compliance. The GDPR implementation experience of organizations has been varied, primarily because of regional variations that come with respect to the different data protection authorities in the EU, regions with proactive and "risk focused" DPA have made the GDPR experience of organizations painless and the contrary holds true for DPAs that have not clearly laid down parameters for compliance and have largely left the interpretation of requirements to the organizations. Hence, the nature of functioning of the future data protection authority holds the key.

3) **Which sectors do you think are in a more mature state to implement the guidelines from a compliance perspective?**

   Sectors which have had exposure to global privacy regulations like the IT-BPM and BFSI sector, are better placed to deal with the compliance requirements of the draft law, as they stand currently.

4) **What kind of challenges do you see foresee for the MSME/SME sector for implementation?**

   The cost of compliance would pose a great challenge for the MSME/SME sector.

5) **What are the key areas the organizations should focus on from a compliance perspective?**

   Organizations need to have visibility over the personal data they have collected. Once this inventory and classification is achieved an impact assessment of the privacy risks would go a long way in setting up the entity to comply with other requirements. Organizations also need to focus on building dedicated data privacy teams to deal with the execution of data subject rights and creating processes to handle breach notification requirements.

6) **What kinds of costs are associated in data privacy implementation?**

   Varies greatly based on the role of the organization and the type of law the entity is subject to.

7) What do you think is the likely impact of data localization provisions on technology and digital services companies?

Mandating data localization would undermine the competitiveness of Indian start-ups, SMEs, e-commerce firms, FinTech and other technology driven firms. They would not be able to leverage global cloud technologies and platforms. This would create cascading levels of distortion in the economy as personal data, in some form, is embedded in a gamut of services. As Indian firms expand overseas, they would be forced to undertake a data residency strategy based on compliance instead of quality, cost and economies of scale. This would also act as a dampener to IT exports, even as it would frustrate the efforts of start-ups and SMEs to look beyond the domestic market.

With data localization, India would become a less attractive destination for start-ups based outside of India. As the financial sector leads innovation, non-Indian start-ups which generally have less funds and might not be localized in India would not be able to provide their service here, before making a capital investment in data localization. Hence, they will not be able to test India market, and would be forced to bring their innovations much later to India.

It is well-recognized that the ease with which cross-border data transfers occur has been a significant contributor to the success of modern globalised economies. India has been a beneficiary of this, with outsourcing and the other services being the largest export sector. MeitY estimated that IT-BPM exports out of India were U.S. $125 billion in fiscal year 2017-2018, growing by 6.8% over fiscal year 2016-2017. For India to continue to grow its IT, BPM, and outsourcing sectors in relation to global markets, cross-border data flows are a critical driver which must be encouraged and preserved.

8) **Would you have any specific suggestions or improvements on the current Data Protection Bill?**

Territorial Scope: The drafting of S.2 in the present form is ambiguous. As this lays down the jurisdiction of the law, it is important to define it precisely.

Storage limitation [S.10] needs to be amended to provide an option to store in a manner that does not permit use. It should be noted that world over, including in GDPR, data deletion is one provision which has been difficult to implement for the industry and hence, the provision should be redrafted to put restrictions on use rather than deletion, similar to the *Right to be Forgotten* provision.

Addition of Performance of Contract: Fulfilment of a contract should be a lawful ground to process data. This ground should only be available when such processing is necessary to deliver the fiduciary's side of the contract with the Data Principal. The data required to enter into a contract or perform a contract should be within the scope of the contract and services offered. Reading this with the larger transparency obligation on fiduciaries, would prevent any potential misuse and reduce burden on consent for every potential digital exchange between the consumer and the fiduciary.

Personal Data: All personal data should be exempted from local copy storage requirement.

Sensitive Personal Data: SPD should be exempted from local copy storage requirements. (a) Additional requirements should be provided under the provision dealing with conditions for cross border transfer.

Critical data: Critical data is not defined in the draft Bill and could potentially have a very wide scope, as in-fact noted in the Report. We can think of critical data in the narrow context of *national security risk* only and in sectors like defence.

Cross-border Transfers: The conditions for cross-border transfer of personal data should be relaxed. This is in line with the approach of the Bill to try and impose obligations based on the potential risks.

(a) The requirement to obtain an additional consent for cross border transfer should be removed. This is unnecessary and in all likelihood is an administrative burden, as the processing (even in the absence of this additional consent) can only take place based on permitted grounds of processing.

(b) The conditions for cross border transfer of sensitive personal data should be limited to:

(i) imposing obligations on the Data Fiduciary to ensure access to the DPA or sector regulator for lawful reasons, and

(ii) ensuring that data is stored in a jurisdiction where such lawful access is not hindered by the operation of any law in that jurisdiction.

Compensation: The act of taking any decision, on a rational basis, to deny or withdraw services should not constitute harm. The definition of Harm under the Draft Bill creates a risk of any evaluative decision that results in the denial of goods, services or benefits of a data subject, being classified as "harm" irrespective of whether the decision was taken in a fair manner.

Penalties: The provisions around stiff monetary penalties need to be modified to ensure that they are proportionate to the violations.

Criminal Offences: The inclusion of criminal offences is draconian and would have an big impact on India's image as an investment destination.

11.2 R Subramania Kumar, Ex-Chairman, Indian Overseas Bank

1) How do you look upon data protection bill proposed for the Indian industry and in particular financial sector?

It is a positive development. The right to privacy is a fundamental right. It is essential to protect personal data of customers / individuals, unless it is shared with their consent. It is in line with the global movement on 'privacy and data protection'.

In Indian financial sector, the volume of personal data handled is enormous. The present system is not sufficiently enabled to protect, due to lack of awareness amongst the customers and employees. The bill will cast greater responsibility on service provider and protect. This may call for systemic changes on the data store and data transit.

2) How do you think it impacts your organization, what specific challenges do you foresee for its compliance?

Multiple versions of the data stored in multiple systems across the organization. Data mapping exercise of each customer (data principal) will be challenging. Segregation of general data and personal data will be a challenging task. Personal data is also used for authentication and authorization purpose. The data needs to be protected in storage, in transmission and at usage.

Mechanism and techniques for the protection of personal data need huge investment, resources and effort. Proper policy and plan need to be devised based on the new requirement since the existing arrangement may not be sufficient.

3) **What are the current provisions for data protection and confidentiality in banking/financial sector?**
    - RBI Cyber Security Framework 2016 and other circulars/advisories.
    - ISO 27001 series, PCI-DSS
    - Information Technology act 2008 and Amendments
    - Credit Information Companies Act 2005

4) **What data protection measures are in place in your organization and in particular for protection of personal data of customers?**
    - Data Retention Policy.
    - Data Leak Prevention (DLP) Solution.
    - Data protection in all stages of data life cycle (Data capture, data transit, data storage, data retrieval, data destruction)

    Sensitive data is transmitted and stored in encrypted form. Database Activity Monitoring (DAM) Solution is implemented to monitor and control Database activities. Sensitive personal data in all view points are masked. The access to data is based on need to know basis. The data in transmission is done in a secured channel. Secured technologies and protocols such as IPSec, HTTPS, and SFTP are used. The DLP solution is implemented in end points.

5) **What are the current data retention policies in your organization and data deletion or data anonymization practices for personal data that is no more required to be retained?**

    Data Retention Policy for retention of data for 10 years.

    Practices followed for data deletion: Data sanitization, Degaussing and Physical Destroying of storage devices (only when the service is discontinued), else it is stored offsite almost permanently.

6) **How important is data analytics to your business and do you use data from outside sources (other than directly collected from customers)?**

   Data analytics is important since attaining 360 degree view of customer becomes important need. Necessarily data collected or subscribed from outside sources are also to be used.

   Data collected legitimately from outside sources such as CIBIL, CRISIL, CERSAI and others are used.

   Bank has implemented Business Intelligence tool which is used for data analytics of business and customer data. Artificial Intelligence and Machine Learning technics need to be introduced to study the customer behavior.

7) **Does your organization share personal data with third parties for processing or any other purpose? What process & contractual provisions are followed to ensure that data continues to be protected and there is no unauthorized breach or access?**

   Yes, we share customer data to authenticated and authorised / service providers for business purposes.

   Non Disclosure Agreement (NDA), Service Level Agreement (SLA) are in place. However, data is physically stored in bank controlled locations.

   Due diligence is followed before selecting the vendors. Right to audit and liability clause are there in the contract with the vendor. It facilitates us to audit the data protection measures taken by the vendor towards our customer data. It is a challenge to practically verify whether data is handled only for the intended purpose at third party environment.

   Encryption during transmission of data is maintained. Secured channel is established with the vendor facilities by implementing technologies like IPSEC, HTTPS, SFTP etc.,

8) **Are there any areas where you see implementation challenges?**

   In the digital environment, the data of customer from one organisation is traversed to multiple locations/touch points. Protecting the same in each level is a challenge.

Implementing data anonymization in the existing software products is challenge.

The concept of Privacy by Design is to be introduced in the data life cycle. It is a challenge.

The data collected for one purpose should not be used for other purpose without further consent by the customer. Organizations need to identify the technology for managing and storing consent.

Creating customer / employees awareness is a challenging.

9) **What kind of costs do you see in implementing data protection and privacy provisions?**

High Investment on Mechanism and Technology will be needed to protect data. (e.g., Data Base with advanced encryption facility, Existing products to be process re-engineered to suit the law).

Human resources with required expertise will be costlier. New roles like Data Protection Officer will be created.

Data Breach will be taken very serious and penalty and compensation will be severe. Legal Risk and Reputational loss will be high.

Compliance Cost will increase.

10) **Do you see any changes in business processes or any tools deployment within your organization for meeting compliance obligations?**

Yes. Existing products to be process re-engineered to suit the new requirement. Business process change will be done to meet the privacy compliance by changing /modifying our existing processes. (For example, existing rules to identify the 'privacy' and proper data classification are to be redefined. The accountability aspects are to be revisited)

Our software and systems need to be modified /developed to meet data privacy and protection goals.

11) What kind of framework, security, and training do you currently have in place in relation to data protection?

Framework: RBI's Cyber Security Framework and other circulars/advisories.

Security: Policy and Governance framework is in place. Exclusive Security team under CISO is in place. Cyber Security Operation Centre is functional.

Training: Senior executives like CIO/CRO/CISO are trained and certified in Cyber/IT Security by IDRBT. Need for training will increase.

11.3 Rajneesh Kumar- CEO, Canara Robeco Mutual Fund

1) **How do you look upon data protection bill proposed for the Indian industry and in particular financial sector?**

   The much-awaited Personal Data Protection Bill is finally out and organizations across industries are evaluating the impact of the regulation on their businesses. While India-based organizations with global footprints have already taken measures to comply with regulations such as the General Data Protection Regulation (GDPR), entities which operate primarily in the Indian market are anxious to understand the impact of the Data Protection Bill on their day-to-day operations. In line with many regulations across the globe, the Indian Personal Data Protection Bill also introduces and mandates the concept of 'privacy by design. Organizations will have to embed this concept in the entire data life cycle – collection, processing and use, storage, transmission, archival and disposal. In short, the bill is in the right direction towards augmenting the data privacy laws in India.

2) **How do you think it impacts your organization, what specific challenges do you foresee for its compliance?**

   As a group entity of European parentage, our organization has policy measures in the pipeline towards general data protection regulations of Europe. The same is under active consideration and will be implemented in due course. The major challenge would be various costs associated with its implementation, which is uniform across and is not dependent on the size of an organization relative to the industry.

3) **What are the current provisions for data protection and confidentiality in banking / financial sector?**
   a) Right to Privacy - fundamental right u/a 21 of the Constitution

Data Protection and Privacy Implementation

    b) Primary Legislation - IT Act and the IT (Reasonable Practices and Procedures and Sensitive Personal Data or Information) Rules 2011

    c) Sectoral regulations - SEBI as a regulatory body to Mutual Funds in India have issued operational guidelines towards protection, manner of handling, disclosure and governance with respect to sensitive personal data and information of the investors or clients.

4) **What data protection measures are in place in your organization and in particular for protection of personal data of customers?**

SEBI has mandated all asset management companies (AMCs) to design and implement Cyber Security and Cyber Resilience framework to protect integrity of data and guard against breaches of privacy as part of the operational risk management. The AMCs are expected to have robust framework in order to provide essential facilities and services and perform critical functions as part of the securities market. We are in the process of formulating and implementing policies and procedures which will include - (a) identification of critical assets, their sensitivity and criticality for business operations, service and data management. (b) access controls (c) physical security (d) network security management (e) security of client's data/information (f) vulnerability assessment and penetration testing (g) monitoring & detection (h) response and recovery (i) sharing information (j) training (k) audits (l) supervision and standards for vendors or service providers.

5) **What are the current data retention policies in your organization and data deletion or data anonymization practices for personal data that are no more required to be retained?**

SEBI Mutual Funds Regulations and Prevention of Money Laundering Act, Rules made there under prescribe minimum retention period, record keeping and handling of the client data or information.

6) **How important is data analytics to your business and do you use data from outside sources (other than directly collected from customers).**

As such our organization does not use any data analytics based on the client's sensitive and personal information. However, we use the data from third-party sources, which is based on the industry data for various internal measurements.

7) **Does your organization share personal data with third parties for processing or any other purpose? What process & contractual provisions are followed to ensure that data continues to be protected and there is no unauthorized breach or access?**

The personal data and information of a client investing in mutual funds are processed, retained and handled by the registrar and transfer agent (RTA), who is registered with SEBI as a financial intermediary. As such an RTA has similar general data protection obligations as are prescribed by SEBI/FIU for other financial intermediaries. A separate contract is entered into with the RTA/any other third party to whom personal data and information of a client is accessible. Such vendors or service providers are subjected to similar standards that are applicable to our organization.

8) **Are there any areas where you see implementation challenges?**

We do not see major implementation challenges since our company and consequentially the industry has implemented various technology-based measures.

Data Protection and Privacy Implementation

9) **What kind of costs do you see in implementing data protection and privacy provisions?**
Technology cost is the major one in implementing personal data protection and privacy provisions.

10) **Do you see any changes in Business processes or any tools deployment with in your organization for meeting compliance obligations?**
We are aligning to the regulatory requirements in this area. Hence, suitable policies and procedures will be put in place for protecting personal data and information about the clients.

11) **What kind of framework, security, and training do you currently have in place in relation to data protection?**
The kind of framework implemented in our organization includes, application controls, user management, security entitlements, business rules controls, interface controls, data center environment controls, access controls, LAN authentication, desktop hardening controls, operating system and database controls, etc. to name a few. Data Protection is part of the IT training provided to the staff on an annual basis.

11.4 Dr Vinay Aggarwal, Chairman & MD, Pushpanjanli Crosslay Hospital

1) **How do you look upon data protection bill proposed for the Indian industry and in particular healthcare sector?**

   The data protection bill is a welcome step to protect sensitive data of customers– however, the requirements and obligations from healthcare providers need to be made less stringent (which presently includes hefty penalties and imprisonment of 3-5 years) especially when there is a unintentional sharing of data by healthcare providers or employees for clinical or research purposes. Currently, this Data protection bill is largely modeled on GDPR regulations for Europe where the level of maturity of all healthcare constituents is very high which might not be fully applicable for Indian context. We hope genuine concerns of Indian healthcare will be taken into account in the final framing and promulgation of the data protection regulations.

2) **Does your organization carry any GDPR compliance obligations? If so, how was your experience in its implementation?**

   We have very limited GDPR compliance obligations as the medical tourism of European nationals is very limited – while we are ensuring authentication, patient consent and other basic data security checks for all our patients, we are presently not having any specific provisions with respect to GDPR regulations.

3) **How do you think the data protection bill impacts your organization, what specific challenges do you foresee for its compliance?**

   The Data protection bill will increase cost of compliance to healthcare organizations and also if the Right to withdraw consent is provided to customers, this sometimes might run contrary to the vision of mandating storage of electronic health records of our patients since deletion of the individual patient information from electronic records might prove cumbersome. Also, the provision specifying need to store all data within hospital premises should be reviewed since this might mean cancellation of outsourcing infrastructure and datacenter arrangements to IT service providers on private cloud etc. in which case arranging all requisite IT Infrastructure and datacenter skill sets within hospitals might be a challenge. It might still be possible to host the infrastructure and data within country with outsourced providers, but hosting it within hospital organization premises, hopefully will not be a mandatory requirement, else will need to spiraling of costs for IT for hospitals.

4) **What are the current provisions for data protection and confidentiality in the healthcare sector?**
   There are certain provisions already for data protection and confidentiality which also include need to assign a Data protection officer in organizations, which should ideally be someone from Compliance team, who understands the sensitivity of data and data sharing implications.

5) **What data protection measures are in place in your organization and in particular for protection of personal data of customers?**
   We have ensured network and perimeter level security for enterprise data with firewalls, intrusion prevention and detection systems with security policies deployed using outsourced managed service providers. We have also done data encryption of our laptops to protect personal and organizational data. We have deployed advanced threat prevention tool on key enterprise servers and on designated organizational users handling sensitive data. We have also created a set of security metrics which are monitored on a monthly basis for ensuring a high degree of patching compliance for critical security patches released by OEMs such as Microsoft, measure antivirus compliance, level of USB and VPN access, and perform penetration and vulnerability tests for internet facing devices and applications on periodic basis. Also, we have put stringent password policies and Id / role-based authentication for key applications to mitigate enterprise risk. We conduct audits and also run a periodic security awareness campaigns amongst end users because insider threats and lack of understanding of security aspects by internal employees is the biggest data security risk for any organization.

6) **What are the current data retention policies in your organization and data deletion or data anonymization practices for personal data that are no more required to be retained?**

We usually have data backup and retention policies for respective applications agreed with application owners and plan the same accordingly. In every case requiring data sharing or discussion on application aspects, Non-disclosure agreement contracts are signed with respective third parties and majority of times, data is anonymized before sharing, as appropriate based on sensitivity of data to be shared.

7) **How important is data analytics to your business and do you use data from outside sources (other than directly collected from customers)?**

Data is the new currency of today's world and insights gathered through data analytics is what drives effective business performance. At Max healthcare, we have deployed singular enterprise-wide systems for Hospital information system, electronic health records, Enterprise resource planning, Customer relationship management, Patient portal, Radiology imaging and picture archival system, etc. all powered by a unified data warehouse, which is hugely beneficial for driving enterprise operational performance, service excellence and clinical quality parameters for our customers. We have our own datasets used for this analysis and usually don't use data collected from outside sources.

8) **Does your organization share personal data with third parties for processing or any other purpose? What process & contractual provisions are followed to ensure that data continues to be protected and there is no unauthorized breach or access?**

The data shared is anonymized and done mostly for clinical research and medical quality purpose – it is almost always done basis consent forms taken from our customers, and NDA contracts signed with third parties to prevent unauthorized usage of the data.

9) **Are there any areas where you see implementation challenges?**
   The biggest issues we see are in public cloud based new age AI platforms where the partners want access to real time data to further refine their machine learning algorithms. We presently tend to have our application databases on-site with all data stored on a private cloud with our managed service providers to mitigate the possibility of unauthorized access.

10) **What kind of costs do you see in implementing data protection and privacy provisions?**
    The costs will depend on the final provisions notified in the personal data protection bills. However, as per our initial estimates, there should be significant additions to be done to IT cost for healthcare organizations if we are to follow stringent GDPR like data privacy and protection provisions.

11) **Do you see any changes in business processes or any tool deployment, with in your organization for meeting compliance obligations?**
    Yes, there will be a need to deploy more sophisticated data loss prevention, anti-virus, and end point protection tools for meeting compliance obligations.

12) **What kind of framework, security, and training do you currently have in place in relation to data protection?**
    We have created a security metrics and governance framework to assess security preparedness by hospital units. We carry out periodic trainings to unit teams and users on security aspects and have a security and incident management team which is focused on proactively monitoring risks and enhance our enterprise data security. We continually track emerging data security threats and work with internal stakeholders and partners to constantly upgrade our incident management and security response for effective and timely resolution of any security incidents.

11.5 Eric Anklesaria, Global Leader -Banking & Capital markets Transformation, Capgemini

1) **How do you look upon data protection bill proposed for the Indian industry or organizations?**

India is finally moving ahead towards having a comprehensive Data Protection Law which is the need of the hour to truly ensure a person's privacy in today's digital age. As of now, India's data protection regime is primarily governed by the Information Technology Act, 2000, and the Information Technology (Reasonable Security Practices and Sensitive Personal Data or Information) Rules, 2011. However, these laws miserably fail to protect the interests of individuals in today's time. Thus, there is an important need for a comprehensive data protection regime, and the Draft Data Protection law seems to a step in the right direction.

As compared to digitalization, which focuses on better consumer experience, productivity and new possibilities, data protection focuses on content, principle and enforcement. Today, the minimal standard of data privacy has created an opportunity set for the banks. It has led to better definition and frameworks, leading to more discussions with different countries.

The 'Personal Data Protection Bill, 2018' is on lines with the EU GDPR regulations. Such rights have far reaching consequences and though, they cause certain problems for the law enforcement agencies, the benefits far outweigh the cons. The Bill, when implemented, will require the enterprises to revisit their policies regarding data protection and processing, and require them to revisit their IT design and infrastructure to comply with the requirements of the Bill, which may lead to significant costs of doing business in India. Further, the bill entrusts data principals with stronger control over information about them. All in all, it will definitely change the way privacy is perceived and practiced within Indian business.

Data Protection and Privacy Implementation

2) **What specific challenges do you foresee for its compliance in the Indian context given the experience of GDPR implementations at many organizations.**

Much of the concern stems from the fact that the new law may require firms to store copies of personal data in India. The law will not only affect technology giants like Facebook, but also companies who happen to have their employee benefits processed in India. India has attempted to create a complex new legal framework for data protection in a much shorter period than it took Europe to craft the General Data Protection Regulation.

The guidelines for the restrictions on the volume of data collected, how it is stored, the purpose of data collection, limitation on the use of personal data and notifications for data breaches are all subsets of what has already been put forth by the GDPR in some way or the other. So, it should be familiar for organizations already GDPR compliant unless we have a major amendment once the bill is tabled in the parliament.

3) **Which sectors do you think are in a more mature state to implement the guidelines from compliance perspective?**

At its current form, the draft bill is sector agnostic as today every business is trying to leverage data and adopt the latest technology around it.

One of the things that good businesses prize is predictability. Every startup is a gamble and adding profound regulatory uncertainty to the mix is not liable to convince a VC to cut you a cheque. The current data protection regime is so far behind the curve when it comes to the way data is actually collected and used now that it leaves far too many legal and ethical questions unanswered. This law should mark a turnaround point for businesses – they need to start taking privacy seriously and it gives them a template for how to do that. There will now be a clear imperative, in the form of penalties and potential enforcement action, to ensure that engineers and product managers think about privacy at all stages of product design and implementation.

4) **What kind of challenges do you see foresee for the MSME/SME sector for implementation?**

Medium, small and micro enterprises (MSMEs) will have to look at alternative options to the foreign cloud computing services they generally use.

5) **What are the key areas the organizations should focus on from a compliance perspective?**

The broad applicability of the proposed law (as it also includes manual data processing in addition to automated/ computerized data processing) means that simple yet robust automated solutions (data management systems) should be conceptualized, developed, mass marketed and become readily available to the masses simultaneously with the coming into force of this proposed law. The privacy by design principle mandates that adequate changes to the IT architecture be made to ensure compliance. This proposition is difficult enough to plan, execute and maintain for large enterprises, let alone small and medium enterprises or individual citizens. Such data management systems being the repository of key business information will need adequate cyber security measures and redundancy backups to ensure data security and integrity.

6) **What kind of costs are associated in data privacy implementation?**

Complying with changing regulatory requirements requires incurring substantial costs, exposure to potential regulatory action or litigation, and may require changes to business practices, any of which could materially adversely affect business operations and operating results.

The cost of compliance is the major hurdle that firms, especially startups, will have to overcome. But provided a Privacy Impact Assessment (PIA) is carried out to analyze how data moves in and out of the organization, future compliance costs can be avoided. However, the PIA in itself is an added cost.

7) What do you think is the likely impact of data localization provisions on technology and digital services companies?

The Indian government has been pushing for data localization in India, but companies around the world have their doubts about its efficiency and clarity. The Bill suggests that the personal data of Indian users should be held by digital and global firms within and processed only in India. But global CEOs have been making a case for how hindering the free flow of data across borders might have 'unintended consequences'. One concern is that the regulations that govern the privacy of data should be able to differentiate between user data and data from businesses; you cannot conflate consumer data issues with business-to-business data issues.

Also, global companies' lack of support for data localization is not caused so much by expenses. It is caused by the inefficiency of what that does to the ability to provide safety, security and analytics to India's banks and merchants.

8) Would you have any specific suggestions or improvements on the current Data Protection Bill?

Even as protecting privacy of citizens remains the core concern of the draft Personal Data Protection Bill, 2018, the government should ensure that it does not become an 'unintended barrier' to India's growth in a digital economy. The goal is to achieve a harmonious balance between data privacy protection and maintaining the ability to innovate with big data plus other latest technologies. Countries from across the world are coming to do business in India and vice versa. If too many speed breakers are put in place, it would make it difficult to extract data. The Bill should end up being a speed breaker and adding to the cost and cumbersome process of doing business in India.

The role of the DPA in particular would be important in arriving at a holistic framework, given its expansive responsibilities. The law, however, would have to evolve based on issues reaching relevant agencies such as the DPA, an appellate tribunal, and ultimately the Supreme Court.

11.6 Gursharan Rai Bansal, Chief Sales & Marketing Officer, India Post Payments Bank

1) **How do you look upon data protection bill proposed for the Indian industry and in particular financial sector?**

   It is understood that at the core of business relationships is trust. This trust is built by improving the management and protection of data held on behalf of customers, partners and employees. We therefore believe that this is an opportunity for organizations in India and not a threat. In India, we have been lacking a clear legal framework and have been operating in a grey area in terms of data use. The implementation of this bill can therefore act as a clear guiding outline in the long run.

2) **How do you think it impacts your organization, what specific challenges do you foresee for its compliance?**

   The requirements for notice, consent and grounds of processing personal and sensitive personal data will force the organization to redesign their core systems, obtain fresh consent, and change the data practices that will eventually increase the cost of compliance. Provisions such as privacy-by-design, data protection impact assessments, storage limitations, data localization and stringent security measures will add additional onus, especially for the start-ups like us whose primary business model is data monetization.

3) **What are the current provisions for data protection and confidentiality in banking/financial sector?**

   In India, banks are regulated by the Reserve Bank of India (RBI) and the RBI through various notifications, circulars, directions and guidelines from time to time, obligates banks to maintain customer confidentiality and protect the privacy of customers' data.

4) **What data protection measures are in place in your organization and in particular for protection of personal data of customers?**
   IPPB have a comprehensive documented information security program and information security policies that contain managerial, technical, operational and physical security control measures. Also, the bank is in the process of being ISO 27001 certified on 'Information Technology – Security Techniques'.

5) **What are the current data retention policies in your organization and data deletion or data anonymization practices for personal data that is no more required to be retained?**
   Personal Data shall be retained no longer than required, to support a specific business activity or legal or regulatory requirement (if any) as per the defined Retention and Disposal Schedule. The person who has collected the information shall not retain the information for longer than is required for usage as per requirement or law.

6) **How important is data analytics to your business and do you use data from outside sources (other than directly collected from customers)?**
   The data collected is analyzed for improving the efficiency, understanding the market conditions, for performing faster and better decision making, determining customer satisfaction levels, etc.

7) **Does your organization share personal data with third parties for processing or any other purpose? What process & contractual provisions are followed to ensure that data continues to be protected and there is no unauthorized breach or access?**
   Yes, the bank shares the personal data of the customers with third parties after obtaining the consent for processing welcome kits, cheque books, third part sales etc. The data is shared through secured medium and confidentiality clauses are placed in the contract to safeguard the data protection.

8) **Are there any areas where you see implementation challenges?**
   Provisions such as privacy-by-design, data protection impact assessments, storage limitations, data localization and stringent security measures are some areas where we see implementation challenges.
9) **What kind of costs do you see in implementing data protection and privacy provisions?**
   Compliance costs to redesign their core systems, obtain fresh consent, and change the data practices.
10) **Do you see any changes in business processes or any tools deployment within your organization for meeting compliance obligations?**
    Yes, it is envisioned that business processes and tools need to undergo changes for meeting compliance obligations.
11) **What kind of framework, security, and training do you currently have in place in relation to data protection?**
    For data protection we are following 3 pillars i.e confidentiality, integrity and availability. At network layer we are having firewalls for prevention of intrusion, at Database layer we are using Data vault (AVDF) and for access related we are using PIM solution.

11.7 Smt. P V Bharathi, Managing Director & CEO, Corporation Bank

1) How do you look upon data protection bill proposed for the Indian industry and in particular financial sector?

Data Protection bill is very much essential in today's scenario. In the era of rising dependency IT infrastructure, the privacy of data and prevention of its misuse has become a big challenge. In financial sector data privacy is even a bigger challenge. Since financial sectors like Banks and Insurance agencies have very sensitive information of customers including basic identity details and their financial status, any breach of data, can affect the customers severely as well as the reputation of the organization.

2) How do you think it impacts your organization, what specific challenges do you foresee for its compliance?

If the data is not protected as assured by the financial institutions, it will not only lead to financial losses but also leads to reputation loss which is a major Operational Risk.

3) What are the current provisions for data protection and confidentiality in banking/financial sector?

At present (not considering inception of Data protection Bill), for data protection, banking sector mainly comply with the regulatory guidelines prescribed by the RBI (which covers all aspects of Indian IT Act related to banking and financial sector). Also, as part of best practices and also to implement standards accepted internationally, banks are complying with the PCI-DSS in protecting the Card data and complying with ISO27001 to give assurance that organization is taking adequate measures in protecting the customer data.

As far as confidentiality is concerned, banks comply with guidelines on Non-Disclosure information by giving assurance that information is not disclosed to unauthorized users. Encryptions, logical and physical access controls are implemented to prevent customer information as well as Bank's sensitive information from unauthorized disclosure, and allow access only need to know, and least privilege basis.

4) **What data protection measures are in place in your organization and in particular for protection of personal data of customers?**

Bank is in line complying with the Information Security guidelines, Data Privacy Policy and also implementing the necessary controls as per the ISO27001 for I.T.

5) **What are the current data retention policies in your organization and data deletion or data anonymization practices for personal data that are no more required to be retained?**

Implementing the necessary guidelines issued by the regulator RBI from time to time.

6) **How important is data analytics to your business and do you use data from outside sources (other than directly collected from customers).**

Data analytics are vital for banking and financial sector industries. The Bank uses the data analytics of reliable agencies/ sources based on the valid service level agreements with them.

7) **Does your organization share personal data with third parties for processing or any other purpose? What process & contractual provisions are followed to ensure that data continues to be protected and there is no unauthorized breach or access?**

No, Bank does not share personal data with third parties. Data privacy policy also prevents such practice. Policy directs that if the use of personal data of customer is required then it should be used after prior consent of the customer only. Also, data is classified as confidential, secret, internal, and public in the information security guidelines. Based on the guidelines, data movement/sharing will be done.

8) **Are there any areas where you see implementation challenges?**

Sometimes challenges are being faced while making the staff aware and vigilant on data protection /privacy.

9) **What kind of costs do you see in implementing data protection and privacy provisions?**

Costs are incurred by the bank in implementing the tools for encrypting the data in rest, data in transit and also in implementing the data loss protection tools (DLP).

10) **Do you see any changes in business processes or any tools deployment with in your organization for meeting compliance obligations?**

Yes, tools are being deployed by the banks in compliance with the RBI cyber security framework.

11) **What kind of framework, security, and training do you currently have in place in relation to data protection?**

Financial institutions are trying to comply with PCI-DSS, PCI-DA, ISO27001, NIST and RBI cyber security frameworks and accordingly staff are being trained through internal awareness training programs or through external training agencies.

11.8 Anuj Mathur, Managing Director & CEO, Canara HSBC Life

1) **How do you look upon data protection bill proposed for the Indian industry and in particular financial sector?**

   Until now, privacy laws in India have offered limited protection against the misuse of user's personal information. The transfer of personal data is currently governed by the SPD Rules (Sensitive Personal Data and Information, 2011), which is significant but largely inadequate.

   The proposed Data Protection Bill 2018 essentially makes individual consent central to data sharing. In line with many regulations across the globe, the Indian Personal Data Protection Bill also introduces and mandates the concept of 'privacy by design'.

   While some of the organizations with global footprints have already taken measures to comply with the EU General Data Protection Regulation (GDPR), entities which operate primarily in the Indian market/ not falling in the ambit of GDPR shall have to make changes in their business processes to ensure compliance with the Indian Data Protection Bill.

2) **How do you think it impacts your organization, what specific challenges do you foresee for its compliance?**

   The Company's existing information & cyber security framework requires Information Security to be embedded in the heart of every decision making and is a part of applicable project plans. Further it aims to safeguard Customer's sensitive personal & personal information against unauthorized or accidental access, processing or erasure by implementing appropriate technical, & administrative measures to safeguard and secure personal data.

   However, the draft data protection bill shall call for certain changes in its processes & implementation of additional controls towards prevention / proactive detection of IS incidents & breaches and also a review of its existing contract with its third parties.

Data Protection and Privacy Implementation

The Company shall also work towards ensuring that persons in charge of handling sensitive & sensitive personal data are aware of key provisions of data protection bill & also the safeguards mandated by Company's Information & Cyber security framework towards safeguarding confidentiality, integrity & availability of sensitive & sensitive personal information.

3) **What are the current provisions for data protection and confidentiality in banking/financial sector?**

   In addition to IT Act, 2000, the transfer of personal data is currently governed by the SPD Rules (Sensitive Personal Data and Information, 2011).

   Further various regulators such as RBI had also stipulated relevant entities to have an Information Security framework towards safeguarding the confidentiality & integrity of sensitive personal & personal information.

   In this regard IRDAI came up with a detailed & comprehensive guideline on the captioned subject in Apri'17 wherein all insurers are also required to implement the Information & Cyber security related requirements in complete letter & spirit. Further the regulations also mandate all insurers to undergo an annual Information & Cyber security external audit, the report of which has to be tabled in the Board Risk Management Committee.

4) **What data protection measures are in place in your organization and in particular for protection of personal data of customers.**

   The Company strives at all times to ensure that our Customer's sensitive personal & personal information is protected against unauthorized or accidental access, processing or erasure, by implementing appropriate technical, & administrative measures to safeguard and secure personal data.

Data Protection and Privacy Implementation

These controls include but are not limited to the following:

✓ Our security practices and procedures limit access to sensitive personal & personal information strictly on a need-to know basis.

✓ Further, our employees are bound by Code of Conduct and Confidentiality provisions which obligate them to protect the confidentiality & integrity of sensitive personal & personal information.

✓ Technical controls implemented towards prevention, early detection & correction of any security-related event.

✓ We take adequate steps to ensure that our third parties adopt a reasonable level of security practices and procedures to ensure confidentiality, integrity & availability of sensitive personal & personal information.

✓ Undergoing periodic internal as well as external reviews with respect to its Information & Cyber security policies & procedures vis-a-vis requirements prescribed by applicable regulations.

We maintain the security of our internet connections & web pages by deploying reasonable technical controls including but not limiting to the usage of SSL (Secure socket layer) certificates while accessing pages deemed as sensitive and also periodically assessing the same against commonly known vulnerabilities.

5) **What are the current data retention policies in your organization and data deletion or data anonymization practices for personal data that is no more required to be retained?**

The Company retains sensitive personal & personal data collected in line with its record retention policy for business & operational reasons or as stipulated by relevant laws and regulations. The Company ensures that such sensitive personal & personal information are safeguarded across the entire data lifecycle & post its retention period such records are securely deleted.

The Company strives to keep customer's records updated with their latest information. To this end, if Customer's see any discrepancy in their personal information or if a part of their personal information changes, they have an option to reach our customer service/ Policy Servicing teams for updating their records.

6) **How important is data analytics to your business and do you use data from outside sources (other than directly collected from customers)?**

It is commonly said today that the world's most valuable resource is not oil but data. Data warehousing & subsequent analytics helps Company exercise true potential of the data generated in course of its business operations. This not only helps in expanding business volumes & revenue but also in business planning and risk mitigation related initiatives.

Predictive data analytics are used in areas such as Persistency, New business, Underwriting & Claims, fraud risk management and pricing of products.

7) **Does your organization share personal data with third parties for processing or any other purpose? What process & contractual provisions are followed to ensure that data continues to be protected and there is no unauthorized breach or access?**

The information collected are sometimes shared with third party for business purposes & certain operational reasons, which include but are not limited to:

✓ Risk sharing or risk transfer arrangements with Reinsurance agencies/Companies

✓ Sharing with affiliates/ group companies for business assessment, planning, and evaluation

✓ Third parties and outsourced entities for the reasons consistent with the purposes for which the information was collected and/or other purposes as per applicable law

✓ To any other entity or organization in order for them to understand our environment and consequently, provide you with better services

The Company also shares sensitive personal information when such information is sought by or required by regulators, law enforcement & other such government agencies or in response to a legal query/ proceeding. This might be in connection with prevention, detection, investigation of any fraudulent, unlawful and illegal activities including cyber security related incidents noted and towards protection of our rights or property.

An Information Security assessment is carried out for all service providers with whom the Company exchanges data & engages for resource alignment, managed services or support. The Company ensures that relevant security requirements are embedded in the contracts for all vendors which involve exchange of sensitive business data or where business is dependent on the vendor.

Periodic Information & Cyber security reviews are conducted in line with the Information security risk review calendar.

8) **Are there any areas where you see implementation challenges?**

There are areas in the current draft data protection bill primarily towards a definition of 'sensitive personal data', certain provisions with respect to user consent process, data localization , criminal Liability & data audit related norms, wherein Company has sought for suitable changes/amendment to avoid any interpretation issues & to reduce the scope of any ambiguity. These have been briefly outlined below as well.

Section 3(35) (Xiii) of draft data protection bill provides an enabling provision wherein any other category of data (other than those outlined in the guidelines) can also be defined as 'sensitive personal data' if the same is specified by the Authority under section 22. In this regard we have requested the authority to have an exhaustive list of sensitive personal data defined to reduce the scope of any ambiguity. Further to avoid any interpretation issues data types such as financial data should further be elaborated to include specific sensitive personal record types such as the credit card number etc. We have further mentioned that in line with international data protection laws the list of sensitive personal data might be reviewed.

Section 12 of draft data protection guidelines define processing of personal data basis a valid consent and further Section 18 outlines processing of sensitive personal data basis an explicit consent. We have recommended that the two clauses might be clubbed together and additional requirements as outlined for collecting sensitive personal data captured therein .It is further recommended that the current provision available with the data principal towards 'separately consenting to individual purposes' might be reviewed and instead have a consent on aggregated purpose classified broadly into two categories viz. a) those which are essential for the purpose of availing a service & b) which are non-essential / value adds while processing of sensitive personal data

The draft guidelines currently do not specifically mention whether data fiduciaries are required to retake an explicit consent from data principals who were on boarded prior to the law coming into force & wherein consent has to satisfy the requirements outlined in the draft guidelines. Further the guidelines should also clarify on the course of action if the data fiduciary is unable to retake the consent either by virtue of data principal not agreeing or data principal not being reachable

Requirement under section 40(2) mandate that the Central Government shall notify categories of personal data classified as critical personal data which have to be mandatorily processed in India. It is recommended to do away with this provision to avoid any ambiguity and instead have this refer sensitive personal data defined in the guidelines

The draft data protection bill proposes a hefty penalty extending up to INR 15 Crore or 4% of total worldwide turnover, whichever is higher for non-compliances noted with respect to processing of personal & sensitive personal data. These penal provisions shall act as a deterrent and drive body corporate to comply with the requirements stipulated in the guidelines. However, making this a criminal offence might be reviewed, as this would hinder business decision making.

While section 35 (1) mandate annual data audits for data fiduciaries, there are other Information Security related audits which are mandated on body corporate by other applicable regulations viz. those prescribed by UIDAI, RBI, IRDAI etc. It is recommended to have one annual audit which shall cover all privacy & Information security related requirements to avoid any duplicity of efforts.

While section 35 (6) mention that data auditors may assign data trust score, it is recommended to have a satisfactory and unsatisfactory rating index instead basis the minimum requirements outlined in the guidelines & the exceptions noted. This shall remove any subjectivity in the overall audit process while interpreting audit findings.

9) **What kind of costs do you see in implementing data protection and privacy provisions?**
Once the final guidelines are out, the initiatives in the area of people, process, system & vendors to be undertaken are likely to have some cost implications for the Company and increase the overall cost of compliance in the area of Information & Cyber security. This will however also increase the overall maturity of Information & Cyber security posture of Company's especially those operating in the Indian context and also ensure greater Customer confidence while sharing of sensitive & sensitive personal data.

10) **Do you see any changes in business processes or any tools deployment within your organization for meeting compliance obligations?**
The draft data protection bill shall call for certain changes in Company's processes & implementation of additional

Data Protection and Privacy Implementation

technical controls towards identification of sensitive personal data, prevention as well as proactive detection of IS incidents & related breaches.

The data protection bill shall also require a review of its existing contract with all its third parties including those pertaining to affiliate marketing/digital impression generation.

The Company shall also work towards ensuring that persons in charge of handling personal and sensitive personal data are aware of key provisions of data protection bill & also the safeguards mandated by Company's Information & Cyber security framework towards safeguarding confidentiality, integrity & availability of sensitive & sensitive personal information.

11) **What kind of framework, security, and training do you currently have in place in relation to data protection?**

The Company has a risk governance structure in place that fosters a culture of ownership and accountability at all levels of management and has adopted a 'three lines of defense model' for the same.

The Company has a Board approved Information & Cyber security policy to provide a framework towards secure management of information assets at Company and prescribe minimum Information Security requirements which all employees, visitors and vendor/ contractors must comply with at all times

The Company further deploys reasonable technical & administrative security controls commensurate with the level of risk to safeguard confidentiality, integrity and availability of sensitive personal information belonging to its customers, shareholders, partner banks & employees and other business sensitive information available with the Company thereby complying with relevant legal, regulatory, contractual & social obligations in place at all times.

The Company further puts in place an Information & Cyber security training calendar towards ensuring that information & cyber security practices are embedded in the culture of the organization and all employees are aware of Company's information & cyber security policies and standards.

11.9 DS Tripathi, MD & CEO, Aadhaar Housing Finance Ltd.

1) **How do you look upon data protection bill proposed for the Indian industry and in particular financial sector?**

   This is very important and necessary step for the privacy of customer and organization data. This will only help in offering better customer service and differentiate the offerings in the marketplace. Customers should choose wisely the safe and secure way of engaging into financial transactions as the whole foundation of financial services is based on trust.

2) **How do you think it impacts your organization, what specific challenges do you foresee for its compliance?**

   This is an opportunity to improve the process of handling customer and internal data for the organization. Major challenge would be to develop the culture amongst organization for 'respecting privacy of the information related to both customer and organization' and 'developing sense of CIA framework'. (Confidentiality, Integrity and Availability of Data).

3) **What are the current provisions for data protection and confidentiality in banking / financial sector?**

   Regulator guidelines on ensuring safe and secure transactions through robust and comprehensive Information and cyber security policy and its implementation - RBI, NHB
   Information Technology Act 2000, 2008 and amendments

Data Protection and Privacy Implementation

4) **What data protection measures are in place in your organization and in particular for protection of personal data of customers?**
   a. Implemented IS and Cyber security policy, based on ISO27001:2013 standards.
   b. Published Fair Transaction policy for Customer and Code of conduct policy for employees and service providers

5) **What are the current data retention policies in your organization and data deletion or data anonymization practices for personal data that is no more required to be retained?**
   We follow National Housing Bank guidelines for preservation and retention of data. i.e. 10 years after cessation of transactions.

6) **How important is data analytics to your business and do you use data from outside sources (other than directly collected from customers).**
   Data analytics is critical while deciding on the creditworthiness of borrowers and collection of repayments. We use additional data from external sources such as field investigation, third party reference checks.

7) **Does your organization share personal data with third parties for processing or any other purpose? What process & contractual provisions are followed to ensure that data continues to be protected and there is no unauthorized breach or access.**
   Yes. We follow ISO27001:2013 standards and ensure necessary controls with third parties through contracts and regular review and monitoring of the services delivery.

8) **Are there any areas where you see implementation challenges?**
   Nil

9) **What kind of costs do you see in implementing data protection and privacy provisions?**
   Typical costs we observe in technology tools and manpower resources to monitor the overall processes.

10) **Do you see any changes in business processes or any tools deployment with in your organization for meeting compliance obligations?**
    Business processes are not much affected. However, overall change management amongst employees has been critical. This involves awareness about information security and adhering to process controls deployed as per policy.

11) **What kind of framework, security, and training do you have in place in relation to data protection?**
    We have put in place ISO 27001: 2013 framework that is based on CIA principles. As per this framework, all policies for information security and SOPs are formulated and observed across the organization.

ANNEXURE 1

GLOSSARY OF TERMS

AI: Artificial intelligence

ACL: Access Control list

AES: Advanced Encryption standard

APEC: Asia-Pacific Economic Cooperation

BCR: Binding Corporate Rules

BYOD: Bring your own device

CBPR: Cross Border Privacy Rules

CE: Covered Entities

CERT: Computer Emergency Response Team

CIA: Confidentiality, Integrity & Availability

CISO: Chief Information Security Officer

CIO: Chief Information Officer

CPEA: Cross-Border Privacy Enforcement Arrangement

DAC: Discretionary Access Control

DPA: Data Protection Authority

DPO: Data Protection Officer

DPIA: Data Protection Impact Assessments

DRM: Digital Rights Management

EU: European Union

FIPPS: Fair information practice principles

FTC: Federal Trade Commission

GDPR: General Data Protection Regulation

HIPPA: Healthcare Insurance Portability and Accountability Act

IAM: Identity & Access management

IOT: Internet of Things

IPSec: IP Security

IT ACT: Information Technology Act, 2000

KYC: Know Your Customer

MAU: Monthly Active Users

MSME: Micro, Small & Medium Enterprises

NBFC: Non Banking Finance Companies

NFC: Near Field Communication

OCR: Office of Civil Rights

OECD: Organization for Economic Co-operation and Development

OTP: One Time Password

PCI-DSS: Payment Card Industry Data Security Standard

PETS: Privacy Enhancing Technologies

PHI: Protected Health Information

PRP: Privacy Recognition for Processors

RBI: Reserve Bank of India

RSPP: Reasonable Security Practices and Procedures

SMAC: Social, Mobile, Analytics and Cloud

SME: Small to Medium Enterprises

SSH: Secure Socket Shell

SSO: Single Sign-on Systems

TLS: Transport Layer Security

TRAI: Telecom Regulatory Authority of India

USSD: Unstructured Supplementary Service Data

VPN: Virtual Private Network

WEF: World Economic Forum

ANNEXURE 2

THE PERSONAL DATA PROTECTION BILL, 2018- Sections & Provisions

Section	Provision
CHAPTER 1 – PRELIMINARY	
1	Short title, extent and commencement
2	Application of the Act to processing of personal data
3	Definitions
CHAPTER 2 - DATA PROTECTION OBLIGATIONS	
4	Fair & Reasonable Processing
5	Purpose limitation
6	Collection limitation
7	Lawful processing
8	Notice.
9	Data quality
10	Data storage limitation
11	Accountability
CHAPTER III GROUNDS FOR PROCESSING OF PERSONAL DATA	
12	Processing of personal data on the basis of consent
13	Processing of personal data for functions of the State
14	Processing of personal data in compliance with law or any order of any court or tribunal
15	Processing of personal data necessary for prompt action
16	Processing of personal data necessary for purposes related to employment
17	Processing of data for reasonable purposes

CHAPTER IV
GROUNDS FOR PROCESSING OF SENSITIVE PERSONAL DATA

	18	Processing of sensitive personal data based on explicit consent
	19	Processing of sensitive personal data for certain functions of the State
	20	Processing of sensitive personal data in compliance with law or any order of any court or tribunal
	21	Processing of certain categories of sensitive personal data for prompt action
	22	Further categories of sensitive personal data

CHAPTER V
PERSONAL AND SENSITIVE PERSONAL DATA OF CHILDREN

	23	Processing of personal data and sensitive personal data of children

CHAPTER VI
DATA PRINCIPAL RIGHTS

	24	Right to confirmation and access
	25	Right to correction, etc
	26	Right to Data Portability
	27	Right to Be Forgotten
	28	General conditions for the exercise of rights in this Chapter

CHAPTER VII
TRANSPARENCY AND ACCOUNTABILITY MEASURES

	29	Privacy by Design
	30	Transparency
	31	Security Safeguards
	32	Personal Data Breach
	33	Data Protection Impact Assessment
	34	Record-Keeping
	35	Data Audits
	36	Data Protection Officer

	37	Processing by entities other than data fiduciaries
	38	Classification of data fiduciaries as significant data fiduciaries
	39	Grievance Redressal

CHAPTER VIII
TRANSFER OF PERSONAL DATA OUTSIDE INDIA

40	Restrictions on Cross-Border Transfer of Personal Data
41	Conditions for Cross-Border Transfer of Personal Data

CHAPTER IX
EXEMPTIONS

42	Security of the State
43	Prevention, detection, investigation and prosecution of contraventions of law
44	Processing for the purpose of legal proceedings
45	Research, archiving or statistical purposes
46	Personal or domestic purposes
47	Journalistic purposes
48	Manual processing by small entities

CHAPTER X
DATA PROTECTION AUTHORITY OF INDIA

49	Establishment and incorporation of Authority
50	Composition and qualifications for appointment of members
51	Terms and conditions of appointment
52	Removal of members
53	Powers of the chairperson
54	Meetings of the Authority
55	Vacancies, etc. not to invalidate proceedings of the Authority
56	Officers and Employees of the Authority
57	Grants by Central Government
58	Accounts and Audit
59	Furnishing of returns, etc. to Central Government
60	Powers and Functions of the Authority
61	Codes of Practice

	62	Power of Authority to issue directions
	63	Power of Authority to call for information
	64	Power of Authority to conduct inquiry
	65	Action to be taken by Authority pursuant to an inquiry
	66	Search and Seizure
	67	Coordination between the Authority and other regulators or authorities
	68	Appointment of Adjudicating Officer
CHAPTER XI PENALTIES AND REMEDIES		
	69	Penalties
	70	Penalty for failure to comply with data principal requests under Chapter VI
	71	Penalty for failure to furnish report, returns, information
	72	Penalty for failure to comply with direction or order issued by the Authority
	73	Penalty for contravention where no separate penalty has been provided
	74	Adjudication by Adjudicating Officer
	75	Compensation
	76	Compensation or penalties not to interfere with other punishment
	77	Data Protection Funds
	78	Recovery of Amounts
CHAPTER XII APPELLATE TRIBUNAL		
	79	Establishment of Appellate Tribunal
	80	Qualifications, appointment, term, conditions of service of members
	81	Vacancies
	82	Staff of Appellate Tribunal
	83	Distribution of business amongst benches
	84	Appeals to Appellate Tribunal
	85	Procedure and powers of Appellate Tribunal.
	86	Orders passed by Appellate Tribunal to be executable as a decree
	87	Appeal to Supreme Court of India

	88	Right to legal representation
	89	Civil court not to have jurisdiction
CHAPTER XIII OFFENCES		
	90	Obtaining, transferring or selling of personal data contrary to the Act
	91	Obtaining, transferring or selling of sensitive personal data contrary to the Act
	92	Re-identification and processing of de-identified personal data
	93	Offences to be cognizable and non-bailable
	94	Power to investigate offences
	95	Offences by companies
	96	Offences by Central or State Government departments
CHAPTER XIV TRANSITIONAL PROVISIONS		
	97	Transitional provisions and commencement
CHAPTER XV MISCELLANEOUS		
	98	Power of Central Government to issue directions in certain circumstances
	99	Members, etc., to be public servants
	100	Protection of action taken in good faith
	101	Exemption from tax on income
	102	Delegation
	103	Power to remove difficulties
	104	Power to exempt certain data processors
	105	No application to non-personal data
	106	Bar on processing certain forms of biometric data
	107	Power to make rules

108	Power to make regulations
109	Rules and Regulations to be laid before Parliament
110	Overriding effect of this Act
111	Amendment of Act 21 of 2000
112	Amendment of Act 22 of 2005

ANNEXURE 3

ISO 27001 ANNEXURE A – CONTROLS

\	ISO 27001 ANNEXURE A – CONTROLS
A.5	Information Security Policies
A.6	Organization of Information Security
A.7	Human Resource Security
A.8	Asset Management
A.9	Access Control
A.10	Cryptography
A.11	Physical & Environmental Security
A.12	Operations Security
A.13	Communications Security
A.14	System Acquisition, Development and Maintenance
A.15	Supplier Relationships
A.16	Information Security Incident Management
A.17	Information Security Aspects of Business Continuity Management
A.18	Compliance

ANNEXURE 4

BIBLIOGRAPHY

1. The Personal Data protection Bill

https://meity.gov.in/writereaddata/files/Personal_Data_Protection_Bill%2C2018_0.pdf

2. Data Protection Committee Report – Committee headed by Justice BN SriKrishna

https://meity.gov.in/writereaddata/files/Data_Protection_Committee_Report-comp.pdf

3. Citi Bank ePrivacy & Data Protection

https://www.citibank.com/commercialbank/insights/assets/docs/ePrivacyandData.pdf

4. enisa A tool on Privacy Enhancing Technologies (PETs) knowledge management and maturity assessment

https://www.enisa.europa.eu/publications/pets-maturity-tool

5. NASSCOM-DSCI Submission to TRAI Consultation on Data Privacy in Telecom Sector

https://www.dsci.in/sites/default/files/documents/resource_centre/DSCI%20response%20TRAI%20paper%20Data%20Protection.pdf

6. Highlights of Personal Data Protection Bill, 2018

https://www.dsci.in/sites/default/files/Personal-Data-Protection-Bill-2018-Highlights.pdf

7. Leading industry practices in security and privacy

https://www.dsci.in/content/leading-industry-practices-security-and-privacy

8. Data Protection Practices of Indian IT/ITES industry

https://www.dsci.in/sites/default/files/Pdf/kpmg_survey_on_data_protection_practicess.pdf

9. Consumer Data Privacy

https://www.dsci.in/content/consumer-data-privacy

10. Guide to the General Data Protection Regulation (GDPR)

https://ico.org.uk/for-organisations/guide-to-data-protection/guide-to-the-general-data-protection-regulation-gdpr/

11. The OECD Privacy framework

https://www.oecd.org/sti/ieconomy/oecd_privacy_framework.pdf

13. Master Direction - Information Technology Framework for the NBFC Sector

https://m.rbi.org.in/Scripts/BS_ViewMasDirections.aspx?id=10999

14. Data Protection Impact Assessments (DPIAs)

https://ico.org.uk/media/for-organisations/guide-to-the-general-data-protection-regulation-gdpr/data-protection-impact-assessments-dpias-1-0.pdf

BOOK REVIEW
MARSHAL CORREIA*

"In today's world we are experiencing hyper growth in data that is being generated and organizations want to exploit the same for commercial benefits and governments for better citizen services and governance. Some say Data is Oil or a natural resource and it could impact country's GDP by few points. However Data Security and Privacy are critical issues and the data ownership and regulatory issues need to be understood and implemented.

This book is timely and relevant and covers all relevant areas around Data Privacy".

*Marshal Correia was erstwhile VP of Hewlett Packard Enterprise Services and MD of DXC Technology.

ABOUT THE AUTHOR

Prof RK Dubey

(MA, CAIIB, LLB, MBA)

Prof. R K Dubey has been an ace banker and was Chairman & Managing Director (CMD) of Canara Bank. Prior to that, he was Executive Director with Central Bank of India and has held several senior level positions including as DGM-IT, in PNB. He has been on the board of several companies and has been a member of the management committee of IBA, honorary Fellow of Indian Institute of Banking & Finance (IIBF) and a member of the Governing Council. He has won several awards & accolades for his leadership at industry level. He is currently Chairman, International School of Inspirational Leadership (SRISIIM Foundation).

Ajay Kr Verma

(M.Sc., MBA, CAIIB, CISA)

Ajay Kr Verma is a senior professional with over 30 years experience in banking & technology areas. He was the Business Head & Program Director, with Hewlett Packard Enterprise, for its BFSI operations in eastern region. Prior to that, he was Chief-IT, at PNB. He has spearheaded large-scale transformation & system integration projects in banking and was awarded as 'Thought Leader in Technology', by Infosys & Sun Microsystems. He has been President of ISACA, New Delhi Chapter and is associated with various other professional bodies. Currently, he is founder Director of 'iTRUSTe Technology and Financial Consulting Services'.

www.ingramcontent.com/pod-product-compliance
Lightning Source LLC
Chambersburg PA
CBHW021404210526
45463CB00001B/216